CONCILIUM

THEOLOGY IN THE AGE OF RENEWAL

CONCILIUM

CONCILIUM/VOL. 8

CANON LAW

PASTORAL REFORM

IN

CHURCH

GOVERNMENT

Volume 8

CONCILIUM
theology in the age of renewal

PAULIST PRESS
NEW YORK, N.Y. / GLEN ROCK, N.J.

NIHIL OBSTAT: Henry G. Bowen, J.C.D.
         Censor Deputatus

IMPRIMATUR: ✠ Bernard J. Flanagan, D.D.
         Bishop of Worcester

September 16, 1965

Library of Congress Catalogue Card Number: 65-28464

Suggested Decimal Classification: 262.9

BOOK DESIGN: Claude Ponsot

Paulist Press assumes responsibility for the accuracy of
the English translations in this Volume.

PAULIST PRESS
EXECUTIVE OFFICES: 304 W. 58th Street, New York, N.Y. and
   21 Harristown Road, Glen Rock, N.J.
Executive Publisher: John A. Carr, C.S.P.
Executive Manager: Alvin A. Illig, C.S.P.
Asst. Executive Manager: Thomas E. Comber, C.S.P.

EDITORIAL OFFICES: 304 W. 58th Street, New York, N.Y.
Editor: Kevin A. Lynch, C.S.P.
Managing Editor: Urban P. Intondi

Printed and bound in the United States of America by
The Colonial Press Inc., Clinton, Mass.

CONTENTS

PREFACE **1**
    ✠ Neophytos Edelby/Damascus, Syria
    Teodoro Jiménez-Urresti/Bilbao, Spain
    Petrus Huizing, S.J./Heverlee-Louvain, Belgium

PART I
ARTICLES

THE ONTOLOGY OF COMMUNION AND COLLEGIAL
STRUCTURES IN THE CHURCH **7**
    Teodoro Jiménez-Urresti/Bilbao, Spain
    Translated by
    Paul Burns

COLLEGIALITY AT DIOCESAN LEVEL:
THE WESTERN PRESBYTERATE **19**
    Tomás Garcia Barberena/Salamanca, Spain
    Translated by
    Paul Burns

THE EPARCHIAL (DIOCESAN) COUNCIL
SINCE PIUS XII **33**
    Elie Nijmé/Kaslik, Lebanon
    Translated by
    Theodore L. Westow

THE EPISCOPAL CONFERENCE **47**
    Manuel Bonet/Rome, Italy
    Translated by
    Robert J. Bolanos, S.J.

THE SYNOD IN THE EASTERN CHURCH **55**
    Joseph Hajjar/Damascus, Syria
    Translated by
    Theodore L. Westow

THE "COLLEGE OF PATRIARCHS" 65
Wilhelm de Vries, S.J./Rome, Italy
Translated by
Theodore L. Westow

COLLEGIALITY AND THE INDIVIDUAL BISHOP 81
Willy Onclin/Louvain, Belgium
Translated by
Theodore L. Westow

PART II
BIBLIOGRAPHICAL SURVEY

THE REFORM OF CANON LAW 95
Petrus Huizing, S.J./Heverlee-Louvain, Belgium
Translated by
Theodore L. Westow

THE ORIENTAL CANON LAW: SURVEY
OF RECENT DEVELOPMENTS 129
Ivan Zuzek, S.J./Rome, Italy

PART III
DO-C: DOCUMENTATION CONCILIUM

THE VIRGIN MARY IN THE CONSTITUTION
ON THE CHURCH 155
René Laurentin/Evry-Petit-Bourg, France
Translated by
Theodore L. Westow

PART IV
CHRONICLE OF THE LIVING CHURCH

"CHRISTIAN CORRIDORS TO JAPAN": A CASE-STUDY
ON PRE-EVANGELIZATION 175
Arnulf Camps, O.F.M./Nijmegen, Netherlands

BIOGRAPHICAL NOTES 183

PREFACE

✠ Neophytos Edelby/*Damascus, Syria*
Teodoro Jiménez-Urresti/*Bilbao, Spain*
Petrus Huizing, S.J./*Heverlee-Louvain, Belgium*

That the editors of CONCILIUM should devote a volume to canon law may cause some surprise. But the reason for doing so is easily justified: canon law and theology are essentially related.

1. We can, as a matter of fact, speak of a theology *of* canon law and of a theology *in* canon law. Someone has said that canon law is "the juridical mode of theologizing". Theology effectively shapes canon law and presents it with pre-juridical grounds for action—the immutable data of the social, hierarchical and sacramental structure of the Church—and its meta-juridical goal, the *salus animarum*.

For that reason, the vicissitudes and the progress of theology have immediate repercussions in canon law. Consider, for example, the possible and diverse consequences in canon law from admitting or denying the "generic" institution of the seven sacraments and the Church's jurisdiction over these sacraments (which are the social means of grace at its disposal). Or again, consider the effect of affirming or denying the doctrine of episcopal collegiality.

Now then, the pre-juridical theological foundation is often *indifferent or generic* with respect to the concrete instrumental expression of canonical regulations. Or, to put it conversely, we must take into consideration the essential *relativity* of many

1

canonical regulations, a relativity made possible because of their generic theological foundation.

We see, therefore, that the movement of theology coincides directly with the movement of canon law. It is in the theologian's interest to know the possible canonical implications of his theological positions in order to justify doctrinally the historical variables of canon law.

2. The lack of complete identity between theology and canon law and the relativity of canonical norms vis-à-vis absolute, although generic, theological norms, justify to a certain extent the distinction between the *Ecclesia juris* and the *Ecclesia caritatis*.

Theology, on the other hand, has been accused, especially in ecumenical circles, of becoming "Westernized", "juridicized", and of "post factum theologizing", that is, of absolutizing theologically the historical lines of action of canon law.

It is, however, precisely the proper valuation of the spatio-temporal relativity of canonical regulations that will help not a little to acquit theology of this charge. We cannot prescind from analyzing and weighing the historical development of canon law in order to determine in many cases the exact theological doctrine. For by failing to take into account the historical viewpoint and the historical data of canon law, the theologian runs the risk of identifying laws, usages and customs (perhaps very stable and, if so, even more binding) with the norms of divine law (which are inmutable), even when the former are at most canonical norms that the Church can change at will.

Canon law, therefore, can be of great assistance to theology in helping it to become effectively more "catholic" and consequently more "ecumenical". It will prevent theology from becoming identified with canonical historical factors even though theology be deeply involved in them, giving them their form.

3. Again, those of a more pastoral bent accuse canon law of a certain rigidity and of being an inefficacious instrument. They realize that the goal of canon law is the *salus animarum*. They know that between the two extremes—the social structure of the Church and the salvation of souls—canon law is a pastoral in-

strument and as such must continually renew its fidelity to theology as well as its pastoral suitability. The social structure of the Church, being immutable only in its substantial features, makes this revision possible; changing pastoral needs demand it.

The very "theologizing" of canon law tends to absolutize canon laws, making them static and fixed with the absolute rigor of immutable theological truth. It carries such immutability over into the pastoral sphere which by definition is as dynamic and agile as life itself. Consequently, we meet with a pastoral prejudice.

Hence, very often pastoral needs do not abide with the fixity of canon laws which rigorously bear down upon them. These needs force theology to deepen its awareness of the pre-juridical elements in theological doctrines as a prior and necessary step in reaching an adequate canonical formulation. Has this not been one of the most striking experiences of Vatican Council II?

Only by taking into account the essential relativity of canon law within the limits of its essential, theological and immutable foundation can the doors be opened to a *jus condendum* different from an actual *jus conditum*. And if the pastoral needs bring pressure to bear on canon law to attain adequate laws, canon law puts pressure on theology with all the force of its mission—which is to regulate and order the pastoral—so that theology dictates to canon law the immutable theological limits within which it can move. Canon law in this way coincides with theology, and exerts its influence in causing it to progress and grow.

4. Finally, the search for, and the establishment of, the correct application of the principle of canonical relativity achieved by the legislator will enable the theologian to see more clearly how the generic imperatives of theology are formulated. These formulations will take the form of distinct and concrete canonical laws in keeping with the pastoral demands of differing historical and social circumstances, from a theological point of view. In this way, the work and study of the canonist will help the theologian discover his proper stance with greater precision.

This auxiliary role will be especially relevant in the next few years before the "aggiornamento" or updating of canon law announced by the Council. But it will be a never-ending task. The Church, in a state of continual historical becoming, should be continually and constantly revising and reforming its discipline with a view to the ever-changing historical and geographical pastoral needs. Hence, the necessity of a constant pastoral re-evaluation of its laws.

In conclusion, CONCILIUM Vol. 8 will try to move continually from canon law to theology and to the pastoral and vice-versa in order to discover and apply the principle of the generic nature of theology and of the relativity of canon law. Our viewpoint will be that of the pastoral evaluation of laws and their adequate formulation in order to offer reflections for improving a possible *jus condendum*.

Preserving the substance of the Constitution on the Church and in its service, this volume aims at helping theologians in "dejuridicizing" theology and canonists in "detheologizing" canon law. Thus pastoral theologians, ecumenists and legislators may collaborate in making the Church's canonical role more attractive and in establishing, in accord with the wishes of Pope John XXIII, a legal apparatus relevant to the age.

May it have as its charge and its symbol the symbol and charge of Vatican Council II: to be "catholic", "ecumenical" and "pastoral".

PART I

ARTICLES

Teodoro Jiménez-Urresti/*Bilbao, Spain*

The Ontology of Communion and Collegial Structures in the Church

The Church as Life and the Church as Sacrament

Twentieth-century requirements in ecclesiology demand, on doctrinal, pastoral, ecumenical and vital grounds, an ecclesiology of communion[1] to complement social and universal ecclesiology[2] and to replace the ecclesiology that has come to be known variously as "juridical", "apologetic", "post-Tridentine" or "Counter-Reformation".[3]

The Church as life is "a people made one with the unity of the Father and the Son and the Holy Spirit".[4] Its unity is a "sacred mystery", whose "supreme example and principle is the Trinity".[5]

---

[1] Cf. M. J. Le Guillou, *Mission et unité. Les exigences de la communion* (Paris, 1960); J. Hamer, *The Church is a Communion* (New York: Sheed & Ward, 1964); G. d'Ercole, *Communio, Collegialità, Primata e Sollicitudo omnium ecclesiarum* (Rome, 1964); L. Hertling, *Communio, Chiesa e Papato nell' antichità cristiana* (Rome,[2] 1961). All contain a full bibliography.

[2] Cf. Y. Congar, "De la communion des églises à une ecclésiologie de l'Eglise universelle," *L'Episcopat et l'Eglise universelle*, in *Una Sancta* 39 (1962), pp. 227-60.

[3] U. Valkese, *Votum Ecclesiae* (Munich, 1962), pp. 11-33. Contains a full bibliography.

[4] *The Constitution on the Church of Vatican Council II*, Art. 4. Numbered articles of the Constitution are referred to in the text of the article.

[5] Vatican Council II, *Decree on Ecumenism*, Art. 2

Yet at the same time, this "Holy Church", in which "all the faithful, scattered though they be throughout the world, are in communion with each other in the Holy Spirit" (13b), was instituted by Christ with a visible framework. It is "a society structured with hierarchical organs", "the Mystical Body of Christ", a "visible assembly", "a spiritual community" (8a).

Both aspects, the vital-mysterious and the structural-social, form "one complex reality which combines a divine and a human element. For this reason, by no ordinary analogy, it is compared to the mystery of the incarnate Word . . . the visible social structure of the Church serves the Spirit of Christ, who vivifies it, in the building up of the body" (8a) (cf. Eph. 4, 16).[6]

So the Church, while being life in the triune God, is at the same time "the visible sacrament of this saving unity" (9c), the "sacrament or sign and instrument of a very closely knit union with God and of the unity of the whole human race" (1).[7]

Diversity in Unity

The one Church, the Mystical Body of Christ, has many members (cf. Rom. 12, 4-5) (7a and 32a). So, within the Church, "the one chosen people of God", "in the building up of Christ's Body . . . a diversity of members and functions obtains" (7c). Indeed the Church is, "by divine institution . . . ordered and governed with a wonderful diversity" (32a).

[6] Cf. J. Salaveri, "Lo humano y lo divino en la Iglesia," in *XII Semana Españ. Teol.* (Madrid, 1953), pp. 327-62 and *Estudios Ecclesiasticos* (1953), pp. 167-201; *idem*, "El Derecho en el Misterio de la Iglesia," in *V Semana Derecho Can.: Investigación y elaboración del Derecho Canónico* (Barcelona, 1956), pp. 1-54 and *Rev. Españ. Teol.* (1954), pp. 207-73; C. Kemmeren, *Ecclesia et Jus. Analysis critica operum Josephi Klein* (Rome, 1963); V. de Reina, "Eclesiología y Derecho Canónico. Notas metodológicas," in *Rev. Españ. Derecho Can.* 19 (1964), pp. 341-68; A. Stickler, "Das Mysterium der Kirche im Kirchenrecht," in *Mysterium der Kirche*, ed. Holböck and Sartory (Salzburg, 1962), pp. 571-647.

[7] Cf. O. Semmelroth, *The Church as Primal Sacrament* (New York: Herder and Herder, 1966); K. Rahner, *The Church and the Sacraments* (*Quaestiones Disputatae* 10) (New York: Herder and Herder, 1963); E. Schillebeeckx, *Christ the Sacrament of the Encounter with God* (New York: Sheed & Ward, 1964).

Diversity does not, however, destroy vital unity: "this very diversity of graces, ministries and works gathers the children of God into one, because 'all these things are the work of one and the same Spirit' " (1 Cor. 12, 11) (32c), the Spirit who, being "one and the same in the head and in the members . . . gives life to, unifies and moves the whole Body" (7g, cf. 7c). Neither does this diversity destroy the social unit: granted that the Holy Spirit distributes his great diversity of graces and charisms "as he will" (1 Cor. 12, 11) (12b), the ministerial grace of the apostolate, institutionalized by the sacrament of orders, takes the foremost place among these graces (cf. 7c); and it is by this grace that the Church possesses a hierarchical structure and is "constituted and organized in the world as a society . . . which is governed by the successor of Peter and by the bishops in his communion" (8b).

This whole people, with its diversity and its hierarchy, has a great mission to accomplish: "while remaining one and only one, to be spread throughout the whole world and exist in all ages so that the decree of God's will may be fulfilled" (13a); the "Church strives constantly and with due effect to gather all humanity and all its possessions under Christ its head, in the unity of his Spirit" (13b, cf. 13a and 9c). The distinction between hierarchs and simple faithful does not imply any division in this community of mission: the pastors "also know that they were not ordained by Christ to take upon themselves alone the entire salvific mission of the Church toward the world. On the contrary they understand that it is their noble duty to shepherd the faithful and to recognize their ministries and charisms, so that all according to their proper roles may cooperate in this common undertaking with one mind" (30, cf. 32c, Eph. 4, 15-16). Nor is any division implied by the distinction between charismatic and non-charismatic gifts, since "the decision on their genuineness, and on the organization of their exercise, rests with the men who have charge of the Church and whose specific competence lies, not in stifling the utterances of the Spirit, but in scrutinizing everything and in holding on to what is good" (cf. 1 Thess. 5, 12. 19-21) (12b, cf. 7c). Consequently, "it is through the sacraments and the exercise of the virtues that the sacred nature and organic structure of the priestly community is brought into actuality" (11a) and the ministries accomplish the same end (cf. 12b).

The Church as Sacrament, a Great Sacramental Communion

From this it follows that full membership of this great communion in the triune God (whose visible framework is "the dispenser of the grace and truth which he (Christ) sheds over all mankind") belongs to those who, "having the Spirit of Christ, accept her entire system and all the means of salvation given to her, and are united with her as part of her visible bodily structure and through her with Christ, who rules her through the supreme pontiff and the bishops. The bonds that bind men to the Church in a visible way are profession of faith, the sacraments, ecclesiastical government and communion" (14b, cf. *Decree on Ecumenism*, Art. 3).

Now the sacraments are "sacraments of faith", and objectivized profession of faith; they are liturgy, and thus a cultual communion; and as social or institutionalized forms of the Church they are also a social, and thus hierarchical, communion. Unless their operation is hindered, they signify and produce, by their very nature, the triple ecclesiastical communion we have indicated.[8] And so the Church is, essentially, a great sacramental communion, born of the communion in "one baptism" and nurtured through communion in the other sacraments, above all in the eucharist.

Hierarchical Communion in the Church

For the ministry of this great communion, Christ instituted within his Body a special body, occupying a special place in its

[8] Cf. J. Gaillard, "Les sacrements de la foi," in *Revue Thomiste* (1959), pp. 5-31, 270-309, 664-703; L. Kruse, "Glaube als sakramentales Zeichen und Sakrament als Glaubenzeichen," in *Catholica* 13 (1959), pp. 200-11; M. Useros, *"Statuta Ecclesiae" et "Sacramenta Ecclesiae" en la Eclesiología de Santo Tomás* (Rome, 1962); P. Smulders, "Sacramenta et Ecclesia," in *Periodica* 48 (1959), pp. 3-53.

social structure: the episcopal college, successor of the apostolic college.

This college is incorporated by the sacrament of orders. Through their communion in this sacrament all the members of the college share a communion in one and the same universal mission of ministry and in one and the same responsibility and office,[9] all together committed by Christ to the same college (21-23), to which he assigned a head. There is then collegial communion in the college.

By virtue of this collegial communion, "one is constituted a member of the episcopal body in virtue of sacramental consecration and hierarchical communion with the head and members of the body" (22a). And also, the ministries exercised by individual members of the college, although these use their authority personally (27a), "of their nature can be exercised only in hierarchical communion with the head and the members of the college" (21b, cf. 22b).

Equally, by virtue of and in its collegial communion, the college "is also the subject of supreme and full power over the universal Church", exercising "collegiate power", which it has to do, in order to perform "collegiate acts", "together with its head, the Roman pontiff" (22b), that is, in the "hierarchical communion".

Particular Communions in the Church

Within the great ecclesial communion, each Christian has the duty to fulfill his own mission or vocation, "each for his own part" (38 and 31) and in accordance with the "particular grace" he has

[9] A distinction must be made between ministries that can be particularized in each member of the college (magisterium, sanctification and organization of the faithful) and ministries that can be exercised only by the college as such (infallibility, indefectibility, power of self-organization and of distribution of tasks and of individual ministerial powers), and consequently between collegiate acts and acts of members of the college. Cf. T. Jiménez-Urresti, "La Colegialidad episcopal en el Magisterio pontificio," in *El Colegio Episcopal*, ed. López Ortiz and Blázquez (Madrid, 1964), pp. 411-521, 459-69; *idem*, "Del Colegio Apostólico al Colegio Episcopal," in *Rev. Españ. Derecho Can.* 18 (1963), pp. 5-43.

received from the Spirit who bestows his graces "as he will": "one to live in this way, another in that" (1 Cor. 7, 7). All Christians, born into Christ by baptism, enter "into fellowship with" him (cf. 1 John 1, 3) so as to be "caught up in the mysteries of his life" (7c). But each Christian while "following his footsteps" (7c), seeks to imitate primarily one aspect of the rich and mysterious figure of Christ (cf. Eph. 3, 8-19), so that the whole Church, through all Christians, "reveals (his) mystery to the world, even though dimly . . ." (8d).

To progress in this communion with Christ, and through the mutual communion of the faithful which results from it, since "we are all made members of his Body" (7b) "and each acts as the counterpart of the other" (Rom. 12, 5), the faithful associate to form various groups based on the affinities of their manner of imitating Christ, in order to contribute more effectively to the achievement of the common mission of universal salvation.

(a) *Communions of the Faithful:* Some, in their search to imitate, be a sign of, and participate in, "the mystery of that unity and fruitful love which exists between Christ and his Church", bind themselves to each other in the sacrament of matrimony, the starting point of the family, "so to speak, the domestic Church", the original human community, given its due place in the great ecclesial communion by Christ himself (11b, cf. 35c).

Others, inspired by their communion to imitate Christ through the evangelical counsels, bind themselves together in the various religious institutes. Yet others, in order to commune more closely with Christ, the active redeemer of the world in which they live, unite to perform various secular apostolic works (34b), working either "of their own accord" (37c), or in direct cooperation with the hierarchy (33c), even being "assigned by the hierarchy to duties in the service of the Church" (37c).

(b) *Local Ecclesial Communions:* There are also other special forms of communion which have their origin in communion between the faithful and the hierarchy, forming local Churches.

As Christ bequeathed the universal mission of ministry to the apostolic college, it is the successors of the apostolic college above all who must carry the burden of this universal mission. And it was the mandate of this universal mission that scattered the apostles throughout the known world, each bearing, within the collegial communion—as we have seen—the saving grace of his ministry and the ministries of the college. Hence the faithful congregate around their particular bishop, to receive his saving ministration, and so the different local Churches come together in ecclesial communion, "molded to the likeness of the universal Church", without this variety harming the essential unity, since the Church is "the body of the Churches" (23b), the Catholic Church consisting "in them and of them" (23a), and "the different parts of the Church are bound in intimate fellowship" (13c).

Splitting up the work of the ministry, however, with the consequent division of the Church into Churches is not always the solution to the problem of exercising the universal mission of ministry. There are supra-diocesan and inter-diocesan needs. The search for a pastorally effective solution can lead the great ecclesial and episcopal communion to organize particular bishops and Churches into closer union and cooperation, thereby producing various concrete inter-ecclesial communions, which eventually constitute themselves canonically and interchange their particular gifts (patriarchates, archbishoprics, synods, episcopal conferences . . .).[10]

(c) *Lesser Communions within the Diocesan Ecclesial Communion:* Priests, according to the bare theological definition, are "prudent cooperators with the episcopal order, its aid and instrument", sharing "at their own level" in the priestly honor and mission of the episcopate (28a, b, c), "bound together in the intimacy of brotherhood" and "the bond of priestly fellowship" (41c) "in virtue of the sacred ordination and mission which they have in common" (28c). This is the presbyteral communion.

Each priest, through canonical incardination, vows himself definitely to the service of ministry in a particular Church, in the service of a particular bishop. And all the priests of each particu-

---

[10] T. Jiménez-Urresti, "La Colegialidad episcopal. Síntesis de exposición doctrinal," in *Scriptorium victoriense* 10 (1963), pp. 177-219.

lar Church "constitute one priesthood with their bishop" (28b). So the priesthood is in itself a definite form of priestly fellowship: the presbyteral communion, the communion of all the priests in the diocesan mission.

Then, each priest receives from his bishop the final canonical definition of his mission, by being placed, generally, in the midst of an "individual local community" of the faithful (28b). Sometimes there are several priests to each community, exercising their ministry as a team, with a wide variety of functions: in parochial work, as counselors to different apostolic movements, in Catholic Action, as chaplains. So their sacerdotal (universal) and presbyteral (diocesan) communions give rise to a communion in a definite mission ordained by the bishop. The greater fulfillment of the presbyteral mission requires the existence of lesser presbyteral communions.

Just as priests, within the due framework of their communion, "make the universal Church visible in their own locality" (28b), so they pass on to the faithful gathered round them the saving ministry of the Church, forming lesser local communions, also with a wide variety of functions, in which lay peope generally lend their assistance to the hierarchy.

COLLEGIAL STRUCTURES

The Episcopal College and Different Collegial Structures

To sum up the foregoing: the great ecclesial communion, stemming from a sacramental source, tends to manifest itself in communion in the sacraments, in ministries, in graces and in the exercise of its common universal mission, giving rise to different particular communions, in which it takes shape and lives. These, being concrete expressions of the life of the great ecclesial communion, must function with the great ecclesiastical-hierarchical communion, dependent on it and in its service—*ordinato exercitio* —as befits each. The manner in which they are to do this must be duly formulated canonically. In this way the different communions receive their structural expression in society.

The "episcopal communion", itself of divine institution, already possesses its basic structural expression in the college of bishops, also of direct divine institution. But it is possible to give more definite canonical expression to its structure and functions.[11]

The other local and lesser communions, which spring from the great ecclesial communion, each with its particular limited objective, as it were, within the great universal mission, receive their canonical structure and formulation through legislative constitution, molding themselves both to the nature of the great eccelesiastical-hierachical communion and to particular pastoral needs. So different groups come into being, "organically united" (cf. 23d): patriarchates, archbishoprics, dioceses, parishes, colleges, chapters, congregations, associations; councils, synods, presbyteries, senates, assemblies of priests; that is, different "colleges", permanent structural realities, each with its own collegial actions and liturgical functions. So the theological term "communion" leads to the canonical term "college". The "communion" with its theological corollaries: "solicitude" (fellowship in mission), "solidarity" (fellowship of function), "fraternity" (fellowship among its members) will adopt canonically the term "collegiality", "collegial character and nature", "collegial union". The liturgical actions of the communion will be "collegiate acts", and the relationship between communions will be the fruit of "collegiate ties of love" (22b, 23d).[12]

Theological Investigation and Canonical Revision of Collegial Structures

Thanks to the homogeneous evolution of doctrine, there is always room for deeper investigation of the ecclesial community and of collegiality. Furthermore, faced with the changing course

[11] T. Jiménez-Urresti, *El binomio Primado-Episcopado* (Bilbao, 1962), Ch. XIII; cf. footnote 9.

[12] For the history of other terminologies used to describe communion and its consequences and requirements, see G. d'Ercole, *op. cit.* Ch. XI. Those used here are from the dogmatic Constitution on the Church.

of history and of particular pastoral needs, one must examine the "signs of the times", through which Christ speaks (cf. *Decree on Ecumenism*, 4a) in order to maintain the pastoral adequacy, in service and structure, of the collegial structures and their operations.[13]

From a starting point of respect for the essential note of "ecclesiastical-hierarchical communion", which applies equally to the divinely instituted college (of bishops) and to the colleges directly instituted by the Church, we can continue to investigate the active aspect of ecclesial communion as the principle underlying the actions of all the various colleges. The existence of a hierarchy with the power of ultimate decision does not mean that the various collegial structures cannot intervene actively in the organization of their own activities. An active communion, which every ecclesial communion is, must be made up of collegial structures—the canonical expression of that communion—which are active in both structure and operation.

Congar has made a study of the influence on ecclesiology in the 13th century of the collegial principle expressed in the Decree of Justinian: *Quod omnes tangit ab omnibus tractari et approbari debet* (what concerns all should be discussed and approved by all).[14] Applied to the hierarchical structure of the Church, its in-

[13] M. Novak, "Diversity of Structures and Freedom within Structures in the Church," in *Concilium*, Vol. 1 (New York: Paulist Press, 1965), pp. 103f. gives the writer's views on the "every-day realities" which new structures in the Church must take into account; Y. Congar, "True and False Reform in the Church," in *Orate Fratres* 23 (April 17, 1949).

[14] Y. Congar, "Quod omnes tangit ab omnibus tractari et approbari debet," in *Revue hist. de Droit français et étranger* 36 (April-June 1958) no. 2, pp. 210-49. The principle is laid down in a law of Justinian in 531, in the second edition of the *Codex*, Caput 5, LIX, 5 and Caput 7, X, I, 23; it was introduced in the *Regulae juris*, rule 29. The popes of the 13th century made repeated use of it, particularly those whom Congar calls "les deux pontifes les plus hautement conscients de leur autorité", the first and last of the century, Innocent II (1198-1216) and Boniface VIII (1294-1303). Congar surveys the canonical application of this principle in the government of the Church (pp. 224-6), in its sacramental life (pp. 226-7) and in its magisterial life (pp. 227-8), describing its influence on ecclesiological theory (pp. 246-50). To Congar's examples might be added the fact that in the second Council of Constantinople (553) (C. Oe. D. 83, 29-30), the principle *sacerdotes decet communibus quaestionibus*

fluence was to encourage the manifestation of a particular communal activity in the life of the Church. Congar calls this the "principle of the consent of the faithful" and it is to be found in operation in such diverse forms of expression as the "Amen" of the liturgy, consultation in matters of doctrine and the giving of advice on questions of Church government.

Today the increasing emphasis laid on the active part to be played by the members of the collegial structures in the Church is in accordance with the emphasis placed by the Council (cf. Chs. II and IV of The Constitution on the Church in particular) on the fact that the task of building up the Body of Christ falls to each and every member—even if to each "in his own way" (30)—and not merely to ecclesiastical superiors, by virtue of the active, dynamic (and mandatory) character of his fellowship in the ecclesial communion.

On the other hand, we must also join Vatican Council II in its insistence on the sense of service and deaconship which belongs properly not only to ministries, but also to collegial structures. For these spring from the ecclesial communion itself and their function is to live it, encourage it, intensify it and extend it. This insistence must lead to a greater spiritualization of the canonical world as its spirit is emphasized, and to a revitalization of the colleges themselves, increasing their pastoral efficacy, which springs from their very communion.[15]

Vatican Council II is carrying out this double program of doctrinal investigation and canonical revision. This volume of CONCILIUM deals with these conciliar concerns; its articles contain an extension of what we have tried to express in introducing the norms for collegial structures within the ecclesial communion, which is above all communion in the triune God.

---

finem communem imponere, which comes to the same thing, was put forward and approved, apparently partly as a result of imperial influence.

[15] Cf. J. Ratzinger, "The Pastoral Implications of Episcopal Collegiality," in *Concilium*, Vol. 1, *op. cit.*, pp. 39f., which contains thought-provoking reflections, based on historical events, on communion as the essence and basis of episcopal collegiality.

Tomás Garcia Barberena/*Salamanca, Spain*

Collegiality at Diocesan Level: The Western Presbyterate

I

HISTORICAL EVOLUTION

Since Vatican Council I, which defined the primatial power of the Roman pontiff and his prerogative of infallibility, Catholic theology has concentrated for half a century on reflecting on the meaning of the episcopate. The maturity of this reflection is evident in the present Council. The priesthood has not received the same attention, although experts have not been able to ignore it in their examination of the figure of the bishop. These studies have brought numerous hitherto unknown, or ignored, historical facts to light, but the priesthood as such has received little specific attention. Until study of the subject has further matured, statements about diocesan collegiality are necessarily somewhat hesitant and uncertain.[1]

[1] Cf. B. Batazole, "L'évêque et la vie chrétienne au sein de l'Eglise locale," in *L'Episcopat et l'Eglise universelle* (Paris, 1962), pp. 329-60; F. Houtart, "Les formes modernes de la collégialité épiscopale," *ibid.*, pp. 497-540; K. Rahner, "Quelques réflexions sur les principes constitutionnels de l'Eglise," *ibid.*, pp. 541-64; N. Lopez Martínez, "La distinción entre obispos y presbíteros," in *XXII Semana española de Teología* (Madrid, 1963), p. 85ff.; P. Alcántara, "Función eclesial del obispo en la escolástica incipiente," *ibid.*, pp. 217ff.; B. Botte, "L'Ordre d'après les prières d'Ordination," in *Etudes sur le sacrement de l'ordre* (Paris,

For our present purpose, the conclusions drawn from hundreds of texts now known and studied allow us to follow a line of evolution which, starting from the complete uncertainty arising from the ambiguities of the New Testament, leads later to a situation in which the first Christian communities or local Churches are governed by a college of presbyters also called bishops, helped by deacons. From this presbyteral college, which at first exercised its mission of authority and service collegially, there gradually emerged the figure of the president or head of the college, whose distinguishing features became steadily clearer. By the 3rd century the preeminence of the bishop over the presbyters in the domain of what we would now call his jurisdictional powers was indisputable, even if no coherent explanation of this superiority can be found: the explanation based on apostolic succession is the usual one and there is no clear evidence of a superiority founded on the fact of the priesthood itself.

The stages in this evolution can be described briefly. We shall say nothing about the New Testment texts in which it is impossible to say clearly what is meant by the terms *episcopos* and *presbyteros*—Jesus Christ himself was called shepherd and guardian (1 Pet. 2, 25). The presbyters appear in all the early communities, and always in the plural: they appear to act as a body (1 Tim. 4, 14). In the absence of the apostle, who was usually travelling, these bishops, elders or presbyters celebrate the eucharist and govern the community collegially.

The *Didache* gives each Church bishops and deacons, always referred to in the plural, who are responsible for the liturgy.[2] The famous letter to the Corinthians from St. Clement of Rome (writ-

---

1957), pp. 12ff.; *idem*, "Caractère collégial du presbytérat et de l'épiscopat," *ibid.*, pp. 97ff.; S. Muñóz Iglesias, "La colegialidad en el Nuevo Testamento," in *El colegio episcopal* Vol. 1 (Madrid, 1964), pp. 131ff.; M. Guerra, "La colegialidad en la constitución jerárquica y en el gobierno de las primeras comunidades cristianas," *ibid.*, pp. 145ff.; N. López Martínez, "Episcopus cum praesbyteris," *ibid.*, pp. 221ff. There is a classified bibliography compiled by A. Avelino Estéban in this volume, pp. 19-57, and (of more particular application to our theme) in the two works by N. López Martínez mentioned.

[2] *Didache* 15, 1-2; note the parallel with Phil. 1, 9.

ten to prevent the faithful rebelling against their presbyters) is not written as from one bishop to another, but from one Church to another—"The Church of God which is in Rome to the Church of God which is in Corinth"—and it exhorts its recipients to obedience so that unity in charity will shine forth, because the bishops or presbyters are the successors of the apostles. There is no mention of the presiding bishop, an omission inexplicable in a document where the principal idea and aim of the writer is the restoration of unity, except in the context of collegiate presbyteral government at Corinth.

A witness from the early 2nd century is the letters of St. Ignatius of Antioch to various Churches, written on his way to suffer martyrdom in Rome. These letters show a certain evolution over the apostolic period in that the figure of the bishop is distinct from the presbyters and set above them: "there is only one bishop with the presbyters and the deacons", he tells the faithful of Philadelphia. He also mentions functions reserved specifically to the bishop. But these facts are countered by other common phrases in the letters which indicate the continuance of collegial government: phrases in which preeminence is given to the presbyters, equal obedience (*homoios*) to both bishops and presbyters—the divine presbyterate is the expression he uses: to the first as to the grace of God, to the second as to the Law of Christ. Nothing can be achieved without both bishops and presbyters. The phrase: *kai syn autô presbyteroi* (and with his presbyters), sometimes added to the name of a bishop, is most expressive, indicating as it does not merely juxtaposition, but that the attribute of priesthood is common to both, *i.e.*, to the bishops and to those who are presbyters with him, those who govern with him, since he is writing about government.

St. Ignatius' faintly episcopal views were not yet common in his day. In 107 St. Polycarp of Smyrna, one of the recipients of St. Ignatius' letters, wrote a famous letter to the Philippians in which the bishop is mentioned without any special position. The heading of the letter reads: "Polycarp and those who are presbyters with him to the Church of God which is in Philippi"; there is no mention of the bishop, but an exhortation of obedience to the presbyters and deacons, which indicates that in Philippi the pure collegial regime was still in being. As Guerra says, although texts of the time do not mention collegiality, they do show the elements of which collegiality consists, that is: identity of authority, plurality of members and corporate action.[3]

By the 3rd century, the function of the bishop as head of the presbytery, endowed with personal prerogatives of government independent of the presbyters, is clearly established. The African Churches (Clement of Alexandria, Tertullian, St. Cyprian) provide the most explicit witness. The collective episcopate has completely disappeared, and there is a corresponding increase in the privileges of the bishop, that is, in the functions that belong to the bishop in person as a successor of the apostles, a functional succession symbolized by the *cathedra*. With this goes a clarification of the local Church as a clearly defined and autonomous entity, linked to the other neighboring communities by the *communio* which finds its chief expression in synodal meetings and in the participation of all the bishops of a province in the ordination of a new bishop. The figure of the metropolitan, the focus for regional unity, begins to stand out; Sees are fixed and linked to particular cities, with a ban on elevating new cities into dioceses,[4] and bishops are appointed for life without being allowed to move from one See to another.

[3] M. Guerra, "La colegialidad en la constitución jerárquica," *op. cit.*, pp. 197ff. Colson notes that in presbyterates functioning collegially the legacy of Judaism can easily be traced, particularly of the college of elder judges whose structure was copied, at least in part, in the early Church. There are various well-known studies of this subject, to which should be added L. Arnaldich, "Las comunidades de Qumram y su organización jerárquica," in *El colegio episcopal, op. cit.*, pp. 119-20, 125. The author explains the collegiate function of the *Rabbim* who form the legislative council of the community, and exercise their authority collegially. Another document, the "Damascus document", on the other hand, shows a *Mebaqqer* at the head of the college of *Rabbim*, emerging from the college by a process similar to that of the bishop emerging from the college of presbyters.

[4] C. Vogel, "Unité de l'Eglise et pluralité des formes historiques d'organisation ecclesiastique du IIIe au Ve siècle," in *L'Episcopat et l'Eglise universelle, op. cit.*; cf. also Council of Toledo, XII, A.D. 681, Can. 4.

But these changes do not mean the end of the college of presbyters. St. Cyprian himself, who is considered the doctor of the episcopate, since he states that the bishop's powers of government are founded in divine law, and that the bishop sums up the whole Church in himself,[5] nevertheless corresponded with the Roman presbyters *sede vacante;*[6] furthermore, in 250 he wrote to his presbyters and deacons to inform them that for urgent reasons he had ordained a subdeacon and a reader, not that he had done this on his own account, but that he had put into effect what had already been *decided by all.*[7] Even as the role of the bishop grows, the presbyters associated with him continue to function actively. In the mid-3rd century the *Didascalia apostolorum* states that the presbyters too must be considered a type of the apostles: in some Churches it is laid down that the presbyters must be twelve in number in memory of the apostles: St. Jerome witnesses that this was done in the Church of Alexandria "from St. Mark the evangelist to the bishops Heracleus and Dionysius".[8]

The historical event decisive in reducing the role of the presbyters and conducive to the progressive oblivion into which diocesan collegiality fell was the physical dispersion of the presbyters after the peace of Constantine. The first Christian communities lived in cities with the presbyters closely grouped around the bishop, attached to him like strings to a lyre. Outside, in the *pagi* (countryside) lived the pagans. But where Christianity spread to the surrounding countryside, there arose the dramatic problem of how to link these outlying communities to the supernatural and visible unity of the diocesan Church. There are

[5] "And so you should understand that the bishop is in the Church, and the Church in the bishop," letter 66, VIII; in *Obras de San Cipriano* by J. Campos, in the collection Biblioteca de Autores Cristianos, Madrid, 1964, p. 629. Writing to some lapsed Christians he tells them: ". . . so that the Church should be set above the bishops and every action of the Church be in their control. Hence there is achieved a basis in divine law. . . ." Cf. *Epistola 33*, ed. Campos, p. 464.

[6] See letters 8, 9, 20, 27, 30, 35 and 36.

[7] "I have done nothing new in your absence. The decision was made because of pressing need and only after ascertaining how everyone was disposed toward it." Cf. *Epistola 29*, ed. Campos, p. 447.

[8] *P.L.* 22, col. 1194.

numerous indications of a desire to stretch the external signs of unity to an impossible degree, either by multiplying bishops, as in Africa, or by gravely compromising the religious observance of the faithful, as in Milan or Carthage.[9] But hard geographical facts decided the issue; the presbyterate was broken up because bishops sent its members to proclaim the Word and celebrate the eucharist and the sacraments in communities distant from the See. From this moment, the collegial concept of the presbyterate entered a period of slow but fatal decline. The 4th century produced a reaction in favor of the tradition in the works of St. Jerome, whose well-known views on the presbyterate have been unjustly accused of deviationism[10] when they were in fact no more than an apologetic for the traditional structure and the expression of a desire for its conservation.

We must now examine the evolution of the presbyterate from this time on, in both its doctrinal and practical traditions.

The doctrinal tradition stems from St. Jerome and follows a line by now well known to scholars, being transmitted chiefly through St. Isidore to Peter Lombard and the Scholastics. The Canons of Hippolytus (end of the 5th century), which derive from the *Traditio Apostolica* of St. Hippolytus of Rome, stand in this line; they establish the equality of ordination of the bishop and the presbyter, "all is done with him in the same manner as with the bishop except that he does not occupy the throne". There is a continued assertion that ordination does not consist in receipt of personal powers but in assuming membership in the presbyterate.[11] Another doctrinal tradition, originating with St. Epiphanius, is emphasized particularly in the works of Pseudo-Dionysius, whose influence on scholastic thought was so important. In the concept of Jerome and Isidore, the presbyterate is of divine origin and the root of all the power of sacrament and government inherent in the priesthood; the episcopate is an ecclesiastical in-

---

[9] Interesting remarks in Batazole, *op. cit.*, pp. 345-6.

[10] On this question, cf. López Martínez, "La distinción entre obispos y presbíteros," *op. cit.*, pp. 129ff.

[11] *Constitutiones apostolicae*, Ch. 16.

stitution designed to preserve the unity of the Church. The work of Pseudo-Dionysius reveals a diametrically opposed conception: for him all power resides in the bishop and flows from him to the presbyters, created to make up the insufficient numbers of bishops.[12]

The presbytery survived in the group of priests who remained in the city with the bishop; after various vicissitudes this group became the origin of the cathedral chapter[13] and of the presbyteral cardinals in Rome. Certain practices remain as relics of the original full collegiality of the presbyters, obstinately refusing to die, though carrying on a life more symbolic than active. Some still survive, such as concelebration, practiced until very recently in certain Churches,[14] still in the ordination Mass, and happily restored by The Constitution on the Sacred Liturgy of Vatican Council II (Art. 57). The laying on of the presbyters' hands in the ordination of a priest[15] has also survived. Another practice which carried on the collegial tradition was that of the bishops sending the *fermentum* or consecrated host to the presbyters in outlying regions. There is a text from Innocent I which indicates that the practice was still general in 416,[16] and the *Ordines Romani*

---

[12] P. Alcántara, "Función eclesial del obispo," *op. cit.*, pp. 222, 252.

[13] P. Torquebiau, "Chapitre de chanoines," in *Dict. Droit Can.* III, pp. 537ff.

[14] J. Pascher, "Relation between Bishop and Priests According to the Liturgy Constitution," in *Concilium* Vol. 2 (New York: Paulist Press, 1965), pp. 14-17.

[15] Its origin is to be found in St. Paul, "the imposition of the presbyters' hands" (R.S.V. has "when the elders laid their hands upon you") (1 Tim. 4, 14). The *Traditio apostolica* of Hippolytus recalls that the bishop ordained the presbyter "contingentibus etiam praesbyteris"; this is now a gesture emptied of its proper content because the prayer which it accompanies is not a consecrating text but an invitation to the congregation to pray for the ordinand.

[16] Speaking of the presbyters of other Churches, he says: "The presbyters, absent from this gathering today (Sunday) because of their pastoral obligations, may receive from the acolytes the *fermentum* which we have consecrated (*a nobis confectum*), so that they may not feel that they are deprived of communion with us, especially on this day." Cf. *P.L.*, 56, col. 516.

show the *fermentum* still surviving in Rome in the 9th century.[17]

But these and other similar indications of minor importance count for very little compared to the central fact that from the Middle Ages onward the preeminence of the bishops has become absolute. Doctrine, following tradition, has jealously guarded the theoretical basis of collegiality by distinguishing between priesthood and guardianship or episcopate, "authority in *the true body of Christ* and in the *Mystical Body of Christ*". This distinction between priesthood and government is today strongly criticized because it forces an exaggerated distinction between pastoral rule and its eucharistic basis, but it does serve an important purpose in indicating that while historical necessity can work profound changes on the behavior of the college, the deep underlying reality based on the single priesthood of the college devoted to the pastoral care of the faithful does not change.

[17] The early councils of the Spanish Church recall some practices which can be considered as a continuation of those ancient practices of the old presbyterate, such as the ruling that the presbyters should say the prayers (the word *colligant* is significant) in order when the bishop is present (Council of Barcelona, A.D. 540, Can. 9): in the Council of Braga in A.D. 572, Can. 14, 15, the presbyters appear as a controlling body, to prevent any possible abuses by the bishop in the distribution of ecclesiastical property. To this can be added the participation by the presbyters in other councils (Toledo, A.D. 633, Can. 4, Mérida, A.D. 633, Can. 4), &the duty of the presbyters to compile an inventory of the goods of a dead bishop (Tarragona, A.D. 816, Can. 12), the prohibition to depose a presbyter or a deacon at the bishop's wish without his case being examined by a council (Seville, A.D. 619, Can. 6), the obligation laid on them to attend the litanies and the diocesan synod. The emergence of special powers reserved to the bishop can also be traced. In the first Council of Toledo, A.D. 397-400, presbyters were forbidden to consecrate the chrism, "as is widely done". In the Council of Toledo of A.D. 527 this prohibition was reiterated: "Let each one exercise the powers granted to his rank, what he knows to belong to the order of presbyters, without annexing what belongs to the supreme pontiff." In the first Council of Braga, A.D. 566, Can. 19, the presbyters were forbidden to bless the chrism or consecrate a church or an altar, under pain of deposition. In the Council of Seville of A.D. 619, Can. 5 forbids presbyters to ordain deacons or other presbyters: "ne praesbyter diaconum aut praesbyterem ordinare praesumat." Can. 7 of the same Council gives a long list of things forbidden to presbyters. This text is extremely interesting both for its content and for the tone in which the prohibitions are expressed.

II

THE PRESENT SITUATION AND THE OUTLOOK FOR THE FUTURE

The few valid institutions recognized by present-day canon law which have a collegial content are inactive and have no more than a paper existence in the pages of the Codex. There is no need to elaborate on this, which is common knowledge and today much in the forefront of contemporary thought on the subject. So the cathedral chapter is but a venerable relic of the old presbytery, and its functions, except when the See is vacant, hardly more than mere official ritual.[18] As for the diocesan synod, the Council of Trent tried to inject new life into it, decreeing that it should meet every year and assigning important tasks to it, such as the election of synodal judges, the approbation of candidates examined for the post of parish priest, reducing the burden of Masses, etc.[19] Its present decadence is obvious. A comparison of the *Ordo ad Synodum* (theoretically still applicable) from the third part of the Roman Pontifical, and Canons 355–362, reveals two completely different worlds.

In the Pontifical, everything breathes collegiality, in the texts and in the rubrics, which lay down that there must be a scrutiny (*habito scrutinio, quae placent, per Patres confirmantur*). The

[18] The cathedral chapter, the historical heir of the old presbyterate, was at its zenith in the 11th and 12th centuries, as collaborator with, and adviser to, the bishop in his pastoral government. The canons took part in the election of the bishop and the provision of benefices, and could even impose ecclesiastical sanctions; their consent was necessary for an order of sequestration of goods or to depose abbots or other ecclesiastical dignitaries (cf. the Lateran Council I, A.D. 1122, Can. 22; letter 112 of Ives of Chartres in *P.L.* 162, col. 130; and titles 10 and 11 of the third book of the Decretals). The prerogatives hampered the actions of the bishop and forced him to look for support outside the chapter: so one by one the figures of the diocesan curia make their appearance. The latest are the chancellors created at Trent, the *defensor vinculi* introduced by Benedict XIV and the consultant parish priest established by St. Pius X; with this the chapter was confined to its cathedral in an almost honorary capacity.

[19] Session XXIV, decree on reform, Can. 18; session XXV, decree on general reform, Can. 10 in *Conciliorum Oecumen. Decreta* (Freiburg im Breisgau: Herder, 1962), pp. 746-7, 767.

legislation of the Codex, on the other hand, has been drawn up with a preoccupation for episcopal authority, and also, it seems, with an attitude of mistrust toward the clergy. The synod should be held only every ten years, and not only is there no scrutiny, but not even discussion is necessary, since this is only allowed in the preparatory commissions, whose existence is not laid down by precept but which can be nominated or not at the will of the bishop (Can 361, § 1 and 362). And what is true of the present juridical structure of the synod is equally true of the diocesan curia, the legal organs of consultation, of anything, in fact, that could be an expression of collegiality: they reveal a feudal concept of the diocese and are seriously out of step with modern life.

For the modern return to collegiate ideas is not merely a theoretical derivation from a collegial concept of the episcopate, but also a necessity in the present conditions of this technological age, in which ease of communication with the consequent rapid diffusion of ideas is producing a universal tendency toward even larger social units. Problems are no longer localized in small territorial zones, but arise on a national and even continental scale. From a sociological point of view it is most important to note the fact that present collegiate ideas are paralleled by apostolic activities based on the institutions of the Codex: episcopal conferences, the work of priestly cooperation in Latin America, the French mission in its present form of Prelature *Nullius,* CELAM, the "Misereor" movement of the German hierarchy, the permanent Commissions and Secretariats of the episcopate, and many others.

At diocesan level the same tendency is evident in even greater degree, because there is hardly a personal problem that will not affect the major part or the whole of the diocese. L. de Echevarría names thirty-seven different diocesan commissions with a pastoral function that appear in diocesan synods charged with matters affecting spreading the faith, charitable works, the clergy, the laity, pastoral action, material good, pastoral planning, etc.[20] The

---

[20] L. de Echeverría, "La Curia episcopal pastoral," in *Aspectos del Derecho Administrativo Canónico* (Salamanca, 1964), p. 242.

existence of such bodies indicates the growth of a pastoral curia in juxtaposition to the juridical curia, with the inevitable result that the present curia will gradually cede its functions to the pastoral curia, just as the chapter of canons gave up its functions to the curia.

Various attempts have been made to graft these new bodies on to the existing curia. But it must be noted that there is not only a technical problem here, but another, deeper, theological one. Within the college of bishops, joint actions of a collegiate nature will be from now on not merely the result of spontaneous impulse, but will have a firm theoretical base in the promulgations of the Council. Can the same be said of collegiality at diocesan level? A close comparison of the sections of De Ecclesia dealing with the college of bishops (22) and with the priesthood (28) will reveal that, whereas the sentences formulating the collegiality of bishops are perfectly coherent and show a definite criterion, those relating to the presbyteral college suffer from a certain ambiguity, with some positive elements and other apparently contradictory ones. The same hesitation can be found in the writings of authorities on the subject. Batazole shows that the concept of diocesan presbytery lacks validity in the constitutional apparatus of the Church, since the local Church can theoretically function without presbyters,[21] while O. Rousseau holds that in extremis a local presbyter cut off from communications with neighboring Churches could consecrate a bishop on his own.[22]

But the Council has not yet said its final words on the subject. What is known of the schemata De pastorali episcoporum munere in Ecclesia, De cura animarum and De ministerio et vita pres-

---

[21] "Theoretically, in extreme cases, the bishop would be able to do without priests (although he could not do without the laity), his only function being constitutive of the Church." Cf. Batazole, in L'Episcopat et l'Eglise universelle, p. 342.

[22] "And as for the rest, it is not impossible to conceive an ecclesiology following which, deprived of its head, a presbyteral college would consider itself as the depository of the full power of the Holy Spirit and would proceed to the imposition of hands on its bishop." Cf. O. Rousseau, "La doctrine du ministére èpiscopal et ses vicissitudes dans l'Eglise d'Occident," in L'Episcopat et l'Eglise universelle, op. cit., p. 296.

byterorum offers hope for much clearer and more explicit tests, favoring close ties of unity between the bishop and the priests of the diocese, defining the priestly mission as one of participators and advisers in the bishop's pastoral care of souls, stressing the corporative union of bishops and priests, defining the functioning of presbyteral collegiality on the basis of a system of representation with the bishop being obliged to listen to the voice of his co-presbyters who at their ordination received "the spirit of grace and counsel to help and govern the people with a pure heart", as the old rite of St. Hippolytus puts it.[23] If these texts come into being, as we hope they will, their new doctrinal elements should produce a more complete and accurate view of the problem and systematic thinking on the subject of the presbyteral college.

At present we lack the necessary doctrinal bases. Conjectures are not enough to give a clear meaning to possible proposals concerning diocesan collegiality. It is still not quite clear whether collegiality is something inherent in the very nature of the Christian priesthood, or whether priesthood is the same in all (the phrase "the imprint of the sacred character" used in the Constitution with reference to episcopal consecration seems to introduce a degree of discrimination within the priesthood). Yet undoubtedly the chief support of collegiality is the identity of the priesthood in all those who partake of it, founded in the one sacrifice of Christ, just as concelebration is the clearest expression of collegiality, and, in a certain sense, the quasi-sacramental realization of this essential unity of the priesthood. The priesthood or permanent office of the pope is not superior to that of the bishop. The Council, by speaking of the permanent office of bishops, casts doubt on the identity of the priesthood and on the very basis of diocesan collegiality.

Neither is it clear from the Constitution whether collegiality is founded on the apostolic succession, rather than on the priesthood, nor whether it can be said to involve, to some extent, not only the local bishop, but the bishop with his priests, as St. Clement of Rome suggests. These theoretical bases which we would like

[23] *Traditio apostolica*, cap. 8; cf. ed. Botte, *Sources chrétiennes*, XI, 38.

to see established, affect not only the meaning of diocesan collegiality, but also the meaning of the canonical rules which will have to give it shape. This is so because these rules will have a different sense and a different aim according to whether they are considered as papal decrees, as the articulation of a certain constitutional value in the Church, or as a voluntary limitation on their own powers more by the bishops themselves, which they will always be at liberty to withdraw.

And yet canonical formulations of collegiality must be produced, or the collegiality of the Church will be in danger of becoming no more than a fine sentiment. Canonists are faced with the important task of finding the technical formulae best suited to bring it to life. This must be done: collaboration is demanded by the times; the present feeling for human dignity refuses to see collegiality become a mere executive which can be commanded. But episcopal collegiality, by giving greater value to the figure of the bishop and making him more independent of the general laws of the Church, will leave a gap at the diocesan level, since what is a legal tie for the bishop can become a guarantee for his priests; for example, the suppression of the immovability of parish priests could become an occasion for the abuses which some, rightly or wrongly, deplore in the Roman curia, to arise in the diocesan curia. The gap at diocesan level left by collegiality must be filled by the same collegiality put into effect at diocesan level.

So the collegiality of priests with their bishop will have to adopt forms similar to those in which the collegiality of the bishops with the pope has been expressed. The explanatory note read out to the Council fathers before the vote on the Constitution on the Church, which clarified the sense in which it was voted on by the fathers and promulgated by the pope, says that the parallel drawn between the present college and that of the apostles with Peter does not imply the transmission in full of the extraordinary powers of the apostles to their successors, but merely indicates a similarity between the relationship of Peter to the apostles and that of the pope to the bishops. In the same way, the relationship of the bishop to his priests must be understood in a way analogous to that of the pope to the bishops, and the realities produced by the latter relationship must be projected on to diocesan level. The pastoral commission which has been announced will have to have a wide diocesan base. Regular contacts between the bishop and his clergy will be based far more on pastoral zones than the present deaneries which have no sociological basis. The diocesan synod will have to function roughly on the lines of the present Council, without in any way touching the principle that the bishop alone is the legislator. Parish priests and other diocesan functionaries must not be mere delegates or vicars of the bishop, but his collaborators with a clearly defined juridical status in this respect. Cooperation, organized this way, will not only result in enormously increased efficiency, but will imply a growth in responsibility, with great initiative allowed to collaborators, and even indirectly, control or limitation of the bishop's unqualified freedom of action. He will not be able to suppress the presbyterate, nor its activities, but will have to cooperate loyally with it.

But the codification of collegiality in canon law in this way will not of itself solve the problem. A basic change of attitude is needed too. Without this we shall merely have replaced one set of laws by another, and the change might possibly do more harm than good, because we would still be tied to the letter, without the spirit that gives life (1 Cor. 3, 6). The new laws will give collegiality a viable and fruitful life insofar as they are considered not merely legal changes, but an expression of what is original and unchanging in the Church operating in the world in ever new ways.

So diocesan collegiality is still in its infancy. For it to mature, more detailed studies are needed, suitable forms must be found for its establishment and guidance, and a new, contemporary mentality must emerge.

Elie Nijmé/*Kaslik, Lebanon*

The Eparchial (Diocesan) Council since Pius XII

As successor of the apostles the bishop is the head of his eparchy (diocese)[1] where all authority is vested in his person. He alone is ultimately responsible to the higher authority of the patriarch or of Rome.[2] This does not mean, however, that he must always exercise this jurisdiction directly, without intermediary. His reputation, particularly in temporal matters, the need to make his lay or clerical collaborators take an interest in the government and development of the eparchy by sharing his pastoral concern and responsibility with them, the very limits of the human condition, the fact that justice demands the possibility of appeal even within the eparchy, the use of competent priests and laity in the service of the Church, the concrete ex-

[1] *Translator's note*: Since the word "diocese" has different connotations in the East from the usual meaning in the West, I have frequently used the word "eparchy" in order to satisfy the Easterns. Since, for practical purposes, "eparchy" corresponds in this article to the usual "diocese" in the West, I have often used "diocese" to satisfy the Westerns. I have always translated "éparchial" by "diocesan". Pius XII, *Motu Proprio: De Personis* (Vatican, 1957), quoted as *MPP*. Idem, *Motu Proprio: De Religiosis, De Bonis Ecclesiae Temporalibus, De Verborum Significatione* (Vatican, 1953), *quoted as MPB*. Idem, *Motu Proprio: De Judiciis* (Vatican, 1950), quoted as *MPJ*.

[2] "The residential bishops are the Ordinaries and immediate Pastors of the dioceses entrusted to them" (*MPP*, Can. 397).

pression of the Church as the missionary People of God gathered together in all its variety around the eucharistic table—all these reasons impel the bishop to share his pastoral responsibilities with others. He will let them do as much as possible, thereby restricting the need for his direct and immediate intervention as long as he can retain the supreme control, require an account of all and guide them. This is a matter of prudence and wisdom, of justice and sound politics. Moreover, it is a duty.

And so the Codex does in fact provide the bishop with a curia[3] which comprises, among others, a syncellus (a kind of vicar-general),[4] a treasurer and an accountant,[5] a chancellor,[6] diocesan examiners and consultants.[7] It obliges the bishop to call a diocesan synod every ten years[8] and encourages the annual meeting of the diocesan clergy with the bishop so that both parties can share experiences and collectively seek solutions for pastoral problems.[9] For the management of temporal affairs the bishop is obliged to set up a council of experts, both clerical and lay.[10] Finally he is also obliged to constitute a diocesan council.[11] It is this latter council that I propose to deal with here insofar as it expresses in a concrete way collegiate pastoral responsibility on a diocesan level.

I

THE OBLIGATION TO ESTABLISH A DIOCESAN COUNCIL IN EACH EPARCHY

Can. 458, §1, 1°, of *De Personis* obliges each bishop to set up a council of diocesan consultants in his eparchy, even within

[3] *MPP*, Can. 429-31.
[4] *Ibid.*, Can. 432-7.
[5] *Ibid.*, Can. 438.
[6] *Ibid.*, Can. 439.
[7] *Ibid.*, Can. 452-7.
[8] *Ibid.*, Can. 422-8.
[9] *Ibid.*, Can. 422.
[10] *MPB*, Can. 263.
[11] *MPP*, Can. 458-66.

the boundaries of a patriarchate. They are chosen and appointed by the bishop from among priests who are recommended by their piety, their good conduct, their sound doctrine and their prudence. This collegial council is meant to assist the bishop in the government of his eparchy with their advice and help.

The members of the council are therefore not chosen by the diocesan clergy, not even in part. No legitimate custom can be claimed to the contrary because the institution of diocesan councils did not exist in the Eastern Churches until the *Motu Proprio* of 1957.

II

THE STRUCTURE OF THE DIOCESAN COUNCIL

The diocesan treasurer and the first priest of the cathedral are members of this council by right.[12] If the bishop finds it necessary to nominate religious, the law requires him to seek the consent of the patriarch.[13] In the Middle East, where a large part of the diocesan clergy consists of religious who do pastoral work in religious houses or in parishes, this clause, which insists on the patriarch's consent for the nomination of religious to the diocesan council, seems to be an unnecessary restriction of the bishop's authority. The consent of the religious superior is not mentioned explicitly but is obviously required as well.

The diocesan council must consist of at least six members. But where the eparchy suffers from a scarcity of clergy, four are enough. All must live in the same town as the bishop or nearby.[14]

Before they take up their function, they must take an oath that they will fulfill this function without fear or favor.[15]

One wonders why the *Motu Proprio* does not mention the syncellus (or vicar-general of the eparchy) as belonging to this council by right. The reason is no doubt that he is considered to

[12] *Ibid.*, Can. 460.
[13] *Ibid.*, Can. 458, § 1, 2°.
[14] *Ibid.*, Can. 461, § 1.
[15] *Ibid.*, Can. 461, § 2.

be one with the bishop. All the same, the bishop can appoint him, and this is generally advisable because of the great responsibility which the syncellus has in the government of the eparchy by reason of his office.

III

THE PERIOD OF OFFICE OF COUNCIL MEMBERS

The members of the diocesan council are appointed for a period of ten years.[16] At the end of each ten years the bishop is free, according to the *Motu Proprio*, to substitute others or to continue then for another ten years.[17]

If, during such a period, one of the members happens to be absent for one reason or another (death, resignation, dismissal, etc.), the bishop can appoint another one in his place for the rest of the ten-year period, with or without the advice of the other members. The new member will continue in his function till the end of that period.[18]

If the end of the ten-year period coincides with a vacancy of the episcopal See, the members of the diocesan council will continue to function till the new bishop has taken over, who must take the necessary measures according to the law within six months of taking office.[19]

If a council member dies or resigns while the See is vacant, the administrator of the vacant eparchy will appoint another member with the consent of the rest. When the See is filled again, this new member must be confirmed in his function by the new bishop.[20]

Lastly, the bishop cannot dismiss a member of the council during this period without just cause and the advice of the other council members, although he is not bound to seek this advice.[21]

[16] *Ibid.,* Can. 462, § 1.
[17] *Ibid.,* Can. 462, § 2.
[18] *Ibid.,* Can. 462, § 3.
[19] *Ibid.,* Can. 462, § 4.
[20] *Ibid.,* Can. 462, § 5.
[21] *Ibid.,* Can. 463.

IV

THE COMPETENCE OF THE DIOCESAN COUNCIL

General Principle

(a) The *bishop* is bound to ask either the consent or simply the advice of the council.[22] The validity of the acts may occasionally depend upon this.

(b) Within his own eparchy the *patriarch* is bound to ask the council's advice only in those cases where the law requires the bishop of an eparchy to ask for either advice or consent of his council. The patriarch, however, is never bound to follow the advice he must ask. The *Motu Proprio*, however, advises him to take note of it when the council is unanimous in its advice, and to set it aside only when, in his own prudent judgment, more powerful reasons would militate against this advice.[23]

Why this difference between patriarch and bishop in their attitude toward their respective diocesan councils? There is, of course, the greater dignity of the patriarchal office. But there is also the fact that the patriarch's jurisdiction extends beyond his own eparchy to the whole extent of his patriarchate. The law considers that the decisions taken by a patriarch in the government of his own eparchy may be guided by stronger reasons which concern the patriarchate as a whole, and which the members of his own council are either not aware of or not sufficiently sensitive to. Moreover, the patriarch is surrounded by other councillors who are more qualified in principle than the members of his diocesan council, namely the members of his Permanent Synod and the bishops of the patriarchal curia.

Detailed Regulations

1. Cases when the *consent* of the diocesan council is required:

(a) When a member of the council is replaced by the administrator during the vacancy of the See.[24]

[22] *Ibid.*, Can. 459, § 1.
[23] *Ibid.*, Can. 459, § 2.
[24] *Ibid.*. Can. 462. § 5.

(b) When the chancellor and notaries are removed by the administrator during the vacancy of the See.[25]

(c) The administration of goods exclusively destined for the upkeep, embellishment or repairs of the *cathedral* church, and of those which provide for the expenses of the religious services in the same cathedral church, is in the hands of the bishop *with* his diocesan council unless a special clause in the foundation act or legitimate custom rules otherwise.[26]

(d) The alienation of ecclesiastical property worth between 10,000 (ca. $2,000) and 30,000 francs [27] cannot be authorized by the local bishop without the advice of the administrative council, the consent of the diocesan council and of whoever has a rightful voice in the matter.

(e) The alienation of assets that belong to the diocese itself or to the bishop's revenue (*mensa*):[28] The local bishop cannot effect such an alienation without the consent of the diocesan council, and without having heard the advice of the administrative council and whoever has a voice in the matter whenever the value of the goods concerned is between 10,000 and 30,000 francs. Below 10,000 francs the advice or consent of the diocesan council is no longer required for the validity of the transaction; the advice of the administrative council and of whoever has a right to be heard suffices.

(f) The renting of ecclesiastical property outside the territory of the patriarch:[29] if the rent is more than 30,000 francs and the length of the lease does not go beyond nine years, authorization by the local bishop with the consent of the diocesan council

---

[25] *Ibid.*, Can. 440, § 5.

[26] *MPB*, Can. 264, § 1. There is here a special intervention of the diocesan council in favor of the cathedral church, while canon 261 of the same *Motu Proprio* leaves to the bishop alone, and in a general way, the administration of the property of his diocese. It is obvious that this special intervention of the diocesan council in no way diminishes the competence of the diocesan treasurer, as laid down in canon 262, nor the competence of the administrative council mentioned in *MPB*, Can. 263.

[27] *Ibid.*, Can. 281, § 1, 3°, with reference to Can. 279, § 1, 3°.

[28] *Ibid.*, Can. 282, § 2.

[29] *Ibid.*, Can. 291, § 3, 1°.

and the administrative council, and of whoever has a right to be heard, is required.

(g) The renting of ecclesiastical property within the territory of the patriarch.[30] When the rent amounts to between 1,000 and 30,000 francs and the length of the lease goes beyond nine years, the authorization of the local bishop and the consent of the diocesan and administrative councils, and whoever has a right to be heard, is required. If the length of the lease is nine years or less the authorization of the local bishop, after advice given by the administrative council and those legitimately concerned, suffices.

2. Cases when the *advice* of the diocesan council is required:

(a) When examining the accounts presented by the treasurer of the diocese the bishop must be assisted by at least one member of the diocesan council.[31] The treasurer must present the accounts every year, and whenever the bishop requests.

(b) When the bishop replaces examiners and priest-consultants between two diocesan synods.[32]

(c) When examiners and priest-consultants are dismissed.[33]

(d) When a removable parish is declared irremovable and a new parish is declared removable.[34]

(e) When an extraordinary tax is levied on benefices, whether regular or secular.[35] The bishop can do this in the case of a special need of the diocese.

(f) When as a result of pious bequests the local bishop reduces the charges involved, because of a diminution of revenue or for any other just cause which does not involve the responsibility of the administrators.[36] The bishop can only do this after consulting those who have a right to be heard and the diocesan council, and he must respect the founder's will as far as possible. The

[30] *Ibid.*, Can. 291, § 2, 3°.
[31] *MPP*, Can. 438, § 4 and *MPB*, Can. 262, § 4.
[32] *Ibid.*, Can. 453, § 1.
[33] *Ibid.*, Can. 455.
[34] *MPB*, Can. 494, § 3.
[35] *Ibid.*, Can. 243.
[36] *Ibid.*, Can. 255, § 2.

canon makes an exception for Mass foundations, the reduction of which is reserved to the Holy See, unless the act of foundation explicitly grants special powers to the bishop.

(g) When the bishop sets up a council for the administration of the property of the diocese. It is composed of experts chosen by him after taking the advice of the diocesan council.[37]

(h) For the leasing of ecclesiastical property in the patriarchates,[38] the advice of the diocesan council is required (1) when the rent is more than 60,000 francs and the lease not longer than nine years, and (2) when the rent is between 30,000 and 60,000 francs and the lease is longer than nine years.

3. The function of the diocesan council when the See is vacant or the bishop unable to exercise his jurisdiction:

A. General Regulations

The diocesan council replaces the bishop in the government of the eparchy when the See is vacant or the bishop unable to exercise his jurisdiction. Within a patriarchate, however, the government is taken over by the patriarch when the See is vacant and he designates a patriarchal administrator,[39] unless a special law rules otherwise or the See of Rome has designated an apostolic administrator or taken other measures.[40]

Outside the patriarchal territory the law provides as follows:

(a) If the bishop cannot exercise his jurisdiction (taken captive, put in prison, sent into exile or otherwise incapacitated) so that he cannot have contact with his eparchy, not even by letter, the government of the diocese passes to the syncellus (vicar-general) or to another suitable priest, designated by the bishop, unless Rome has decided differently. The deputy then has *ipso jure* (by right) the powers, rights and duties of a vicar-general.

[37] *Ibid.*, Can. 263, § 1.
[38] *Ibid.*, Can. 291, § 2.
[39] In conformity with *MPP*, Can. 469.
[40] *Ibid.*, Can. 458, § 2; 469.

On occasion, and for a grave reason, the bishop may designate several priests who would govern the eparchy in succession. If no such deputy can be found or if they are all impeded, it is up to the diocesan council to appoint a diocesan administrator.[41]

(b) During a vacancy, when the See has fallen vacant the diocesan council must, within eight days of notification of the vacancy, elect an administrator who will govern the diocese in its stead.

B. Special Regulations

(a) If, for whatever reason, the diocesan council has failed to elect an administrator within the required time limit, the appointment of the administrator passes to the patriarch when the eparchy is within a patriarchate (if this patriarch does not already have this power due to the very fact that there is a vacancy);[42] outside the patriarchates, the appointment passes into the hands of the metropolitan, the archbishop or the first residential bishop (in order of precedence), or to the first metropolitan.[43] When an eparchy is vacant which does not come under a patriarch, archbishop or metropolitan, the metropolitan[44] appoints the administrator if the diocesan council has failed to elect one within the required eight days.[45]

The diocesan council must inform the Holy See as soon as possible of the bishop's death, and the administrator elected by that council must inform Rome of his election.[46]

(b) *Procedure for the Election of an Administrator:* The

[41] In accordance with *ibid.,* Can. 467, § 1, and save the regulation laid down in Can. 249, § 1, 4° (the passing of the nomination into the hands of Rome, when, practically speaking, a month has passed without an administrator having been appointed).

[42] In accordance with *ibid.,* Can. 249, § 1, 3°.

[43] According to the various cases envisaged by *ibid.,* Can. 470, § 2.

[44] Pointed out in *ibid.,* Can. 323.

[45] *Ibid.,* Can. 470, § 3. This concerns the nearest metropolitan designated by bishops not under a patriarch, archbishop or metropolitan, with the approval of the Holy See, to fill for them the function of a metropolitan in common law with a certain amount of stability.

[46] *Ibid.,* Can. 470, § 4.

diocesan council must elect that administrator collectively.[47] The validity of the election requires an absolute majority of the votes, not counting those that are null and void.[48]

(c) *The Powers of the Diocesan Council:*[49] During the vacancy of the See, and without infringing certain legal prohibitions, the ordinary jurisdiction of the bishop in matters spiritual and temporal passes, before an administrator has been appointed, into the hands of the patriarch, unless there is a special law; outside patriarchal territory it goes to the diocesan council. Once the administrator has been appointed he has the same powers as the bishop. Therefore, the diocesan council and then the administrator of this vacant diocese enjoy all the powers enumerated in canon 434, § 2.[50]

Nevertheless, no innovations may be introduced; neither the administrator nor the diocesan council may do anything that might prejudice the rights of either the eparchy or the bishop; finally, neither the administrator, nor the diocesan council, nor any other person, cleric or lay, may take away, destroy, hide or interfere with the documents of the episcopal curia.

But in appointing an administrator to a vacant diocese, neither the patriarch nor the diocesan council may reserve any part of the jurisdiction to themselves, nor put a limit to the exercise of his function, nor impose any other restrictions.

When the administrator of the vacant eparchy has been appointed by the patriarch, he must first make a profession of faith before the patriarch and he can exercise the jurisdiction thus obtained only after having presented the patriarch's letter of appointment to the diocesan council. After this, and as soon as possible, he must acquaint all the clergy of his diocese with this letter of appointment. But when the administrator has been elected by the

---

[47] In accordance with *ibid.*, Can. 102-4, with due regard to the special provisions of ch. VII, Can. 467-82.

[48] *Ibid.*, Can. 471, § 1.

[49] *Ibid.*, Can 473-6.

[50] *Ibid.* The usual powers granted to the local bishop as well as those apostolic or patriarchal rescripts granted to the bishop or whoever governed the eparchy before.

diocesan council and has made his profession of faith, the jurisdiction is his immediately and no further confirmation is necessary.

(d) *The Dismissal and Resignation of the Administrator:*[51] The
dismissal of an administrator of a vacant eparchy who has been
elected by the diocesan council is reserved to the See of Rome.
If he resigns, the act of resignation must be presented to the diocesan council in the proper form, but the council's acceptance is
not required for its validity. The appointment of a new administrator after the resignation, death or dismissal of the previous one
belongs to the diocesan council.[53]

(e) *The Treasurer and the Diocesan Council during the
Vacancy of the See:*[54] Unless the patriarch or the diocesan council
has decided otherwise the treasurer takes over the administration of the property which the vacancy of the See has left without
an administrator. The resignation of a treasurer must be presented
to the patriarch or the diocesan council in the proper form. The
validity of this resignation *does* require acceptance by the patriarch, who must hear the advice of the Permanent Synod, but
does *not* require acceptance by the diocesan council. Outside the
patriarchates the election or nomination of the new treasurer belongs to the diocesan council and is decided by absolute majority.
Inside a patriarchate it belongs to the patriarch with the consent
of those bishops who hold office with residence in the curia.

(f) *When the new bishop assumes his office,* he must demand
of the diocesan council or administrator, the treasurer and other
clergy who have held office during the vacancy, an account of
their office, jurisdiction, administration or any other function
which they have held in the eparchy. These same persons must
also give an account to the new bishop of such written documents
as are related to the Church and which have reached them during the vacancy of the See.[55]

---

[51] *Ibid.,* Can. 480.
[53] To be done in accordance with *ibid.,* Can. 470.
[54] *Ibid.,* Can. 481.
[55] *Ibid.,* Can. 482.

4. Intervention of the Diocesan Council in other Circumstances:

(a) Residential bishops inaugurate canonically the administration of their eparchy by presenting the apostolic or patriarchal letter of their appointment to the diocesan council.[56] The same holds for a bishop coadjutor when he assumes office.[57]

(b) The members of the diocesan council are by right members of the diocesan synod.[58]

(c) During the vacancy of the See, the first member of the diocesan council keeps the second key of the chest of secret documents in episcopal curia.[59] This chest can be opened during the vacancy only by the administrator in case of urgent necessity and in the presence of two members of the diocesan council.[60]

(d) In matters of judicial procedure the function of the diocesan council extends to the following cases:

The bishop must seek the advice of the diocesan council when he has to replace diocesan judges who have died or resigned for whatever reason between two diocesan synods.[61]

Unless he thinks it better to do without, the bishop must seek the council's advice when he wants to dismiss a diocesan judge.[62]

For the dismissal or suspension of cursors and apparitors in the service of the court, the administrator of a vacant eparchy must have the consent of the diocesan council.[63]

In order to sue in the name of the cathedral church or the episcopal residence, the local bishop must seek the advice or ask for the consent of the diocesan council or the administrative council whenever the subject of the action is a sum of money which would have required their advice or consent if it had been a matter of alienation.[64]

[56] *Ibid.*, Can. 397, § 3.
[57] *Ibid.*, Can. 419, § 2.
[58] *Ibid.*, Can. 342, § 1, 2°.
[59] *Ibid.*, Can. 448, § 2.
[60] *Ibid.*, Can. 449, § 1.
[61] *MPJ*, Can. 42.
[62] *Ibid.*, Can. 44.
[63] *Ibid.*, Can. 69, § 2, 2°.
[64] *Ibid.*, Can. 168, § 1.

V
The Diocesan Council and the Cathedral Chapter

In some Churches of the Byzantine rite (Rumanian or Ruthenian) there exists the institution of a chapter of canons of the cathedral church. The synods of these Churches have legislated on this point. The *Motu Proprio: De Personis* refers to this special law[65] and sanctions it in canon 465, § 3. Canon 464 assimilates the chapter to the diocesan council in all that concerns the council in matters of diocesan government, whether the See is occupied, impeded or vacant.

The solemn celebration of the liturgy in the cathedral church, the relations between chapter and cathedral church generally and the relations of rights and duties between the chapter and the cathedral parish priest (if the cathedral is a parish church) are regulated in detail by canon 466.

Conclusion

The Future

The conciliar Decree on the Catholic Eastern Churches, promulgated on November 21, 1964 during the closing ceremony of the third session of Vatican Council II, will be the starting point of many reforms in current Oriental Canon Law, now ruled by *Motu Proprio*,[66] and also in other projects which still have to be brought up to date and published. The commissions in charge of the drafting and revising of canonical texts will have to take their cue from the theological and disciplinary data provided by Vatican Council II. The Church of Vatican II is deeply influenced by ecumenism and episcopal collegiality. Insofar as Oriental Law and the relations of the curia with the Eastern Churches are con-

[65] The provincial synod of Alba, Julia and Fagaras in 1872, tit. II, ch. V; the same in 1882, tit. II; the Ruthenian synod of 1891, tit. VII, ch. IV, 1.

[66] Marriage, 1949; legal actions, 1950; religious, temporal goods and meaning of the words, 1952; persons, 1957.

cerned, the reforms in formulation and attitude point mainly in the direction of greater internal autonomy based on the patriarchate and the synod.

The conciliar Decree on the Catholic Oriental Churches has, indeed, recognized (Art. 9) that the patriarch and his synod are normally the highest authority in all that concerns his patriarchate. Insofar as the texts are concerned which treat of the diocesan council, and other texts, too, the clauses which mention "within a patriarchate" and "outside a patriarchate" will have to be amended in the sense of Art. 7c of the decree where it is laid down that "in all the places situated outside the patriarchal territory where a bishop of whatever rite is established, this bishop will be deemed a member of the patriarchal hierarchy of that rite, according to the norms of the law". In the same way the assimilation, on the level of discipline, of major archbishops to patriarchs, the principle of which has been expressed in Art. 10 of the same decree, will lead to other amendments.

As in the whole of society, so in the Church the future points in the direction of collegiate responsibility and decentralization. The hard lessons of history on the abuse of personal power at every level of the hierarchy cannot be ignored.

Manuel Bonet/*Rome, Italy*

The Episcopal Conference

The theme of episcopal collegiality emerged with such distinctive features in Vatican Council II that to view it within a purely historico-juridical framework whose foundation would be the mere evolution of canonical discipline involves some risk. It could easily distort the spirit which at this present moment in the life of the Church animates episcopal conferences.

Let it suffice to recall that the canonical regulations in force since 1918 express that sense of collegial pastoral solicitude which from earliest times has always been present in the Church. This helps to explain the continued practice of summoning particular councils which the Code, careful to avoid ratifying the civil juridical categories of the State as ecclesiastical structures, divides into provincial (those recurring most constantly in tradition) and plenary (for regions comprising more than an ecclesiastical province, be they national or not).

On the other hand, as early as the 19th century, regional and even national conferences of bishops began to function as a matter of fact. These were incorporated into the structure of the Church (Can. 292) for the first time in history and received a very limited juridical status.

The following remarks aim at presenting in a modest way a preliminary point of view. It may help to shed light on future and imminent legislation and to keep the canonical regulations concerning episcopal conferences within the scope of the teaching and spirit of Vatican Council II.

We believe the Council has manifested a pastoral concern, one which our contemporary situation makes most acute, as well as a spirit of collegiality which the Holy Spirit has breathed into the theology of the episcopate, putting the final touches to an issue that even Vatican Council I left unsettled.

The Constitution on the Sacred Liturgy

The legislation of the Code did not move beyond the fundamental bases for action noted above. The acutal precedents of existing conferences of bishops lacked all legislative power and enjoyed only a moral authority. This initiated the custom of collective action. By degrees, this tended to make councils less frequent and resulted in more painstaking measures in summoning conferences. At the same time, however, there was a certain reluctance to endow with binding force the agreements reached in episcopal conferences. This can be seen from a simple reading of the schema of the Council's decree *De pastorali Episcoporum munere.*

Though formulated cautiously, article 22 of the Council's *Constitution on the Sacred Liturgy* was directed at collegiate action and probably brought it about that, for the first time in the Church, universal action prompted particular legislative activity in collegial form outside of a council.

This was strengthened by the fact, marginal to the Council, that conferences of bishops met during the three sessions of the Council held thus far. Though directly lacking juridical effects, this greatly helped to instruct the bishops in the manner of conducting their conferences and, at least in some countries, even contributed more than a little to their juridical structure.

Theological Basis

Withal, the most fundamental basis of episcopal conferences where its theological source can be found has been the conciliar

Constitution on the Church. Although episcopal collegiality by divine right belongs to the whole body of bishops extended throughout the world with the successor of Peter as its head, from the teaching contained in chapter III of the Constitution on the Church flow certain principles that shed light on the restricted function of collegiality.

The Constitution on the Church affirms that the ancient councils in general, even the non-ecumenical, and the communion that the bishops have always had with one another "are already an indication of the collegiate character and aspect of the episcopal order". Thus it can be said that bishops' conferences are at least a sign of episcopal collegiality, just as undoubtedly is the action of a number of bishops consecrating at the elevation of a bishop.

It will suffice to reproduce the following lines from the Constitution on the Church: "This collegial union is apparent also in the mutual relations of the individual bishops with particular Churches and with the universal Church." In a word, positive law, which has regulated particular councils and which in the immediate future will continue to regulate the conferences of bishops, is a concrete application (changeable to be sure, but actual), of that solicitude for the universal Church which, by divine institution, is the concern of all the members of the college of bishops, as Pius XII himself had already recalled in the encyclical *Fidei donum*.

Furthermore, the Constitution on the Church expressly states: "And finally, the bishops, in a universal fellowship of charity, should gladly extend their fraternal aid to other Churches, especially to neighboring and more needy dioceses in accordance with the venerable example of antiquity." It continues: "By divine Providence it has come about that various Churches, established in various places by the apostles and their successors, have in the course of time coalesced into several groups, organically united . . ." and concludes with the solemn affirmation: "In like manner the episcopal bodies of today are in a position to render a manifold and fruitful assistance, so that this collegiate feeling may be put into practical application."

Positive Law

The document of Vatican Council II that will constitute the founding charter of episcopal conferences will be, beyond a doubt, chapter III of the proposed conciliar decree *De pastorali Episcoporum munere.* In it, after making mention of the historical antecedents already referred to, the Council manifests its desire that the venerable tradition of particular councils be continued. Though making reference to canonical legislation, it does not set down concrete norms but indicates that this legislation should be adapted to the circumstances of our time.

The decree immediately goes on to establish the basic canonical rules for episcopal conferences, but not without first asserting the great importance of these conferences for our day, and calls to mind as well the experience already gained in some countries. The Council solemnly affirms: "This Most Holy Synod is convinced that forceful steps should be taken to convene throughout the world regional and national meetings of bishops. Thus, coming together at certain fixed times and sharing with one another the fruit of their experience and foresight, they may advise one another as they form a vigorous and holy alliance for the benefit of the entire Church."

Spirit of Renewal

Thus far we have spoken of the strides made through the work of the Council compared to the situation which immediately preceded it. But complementing all of this must be the spirit that animates the Church in the present conciliar moment in view of the fact that this spirit should greatly influence the molding of juridical norms and even the organization of the structures.

Only in this way can we avoid considering the juridical dimension as something isolated from the other dimensions of ecclesial life. The truly juridical provides the framework for the normative in a polarity whose aim it is to facilitate the life of the person within the community. In its turn, it reduces structures to a subservient role, making more visible and more real that aspect of *diakonia* or ministry which holds good for every office in the Church.

Basic Juridical Problem

What we have said thus far leads us to tackle the fundamental canonical problem that future canonical legislation itself cannot skirt in determining the course of collegiate episcopal action. We would formulate this problem modestly by stating that, before undertaking the task of reforming the Code, there is an urgent and pressing need to set up clearly, in the light of the theological and pastoral teaching of the Council, what we could call in Latin: *lineamenta fundamentalia constitutionis Ecclesiae hodiernis rerum adiunctis accomodatae* (the basic features of the structure of the Church adapted to contemporary circumstances).

Only in this way can we avoid the danger of an illusion that would easily lead to a superficial reform. Such a reform could frustrate the pastoral efficacy which it aims at giving to the positive laws of the Church. The point of reference should undoubtedly be the Constitution on the Church. But the entire panorama of today's apostolate should, in turn, also be borne in mind as well as those ethico-juridical postulates touching on the human person. These are in no way diminished when they are reevaluated in the light of salvation history.

Admitting for this reason all the valid elements of existing positive law which cannot be contested, our procedure should be one of internal dynamism along the lines indicated by the pope to the Commission for Liturgical Reform: "Let all innovations be related to and in keeping with sound tradition and any new forms adopted should in some way grow organically from forms already existing." These new forms must be reached through reflection motivated by pastoral solicitude and illumined by faith as well as by the natural principles of ethics. It is not simply a matter of combining the norms of yesterday with those of today, but rather of passing from the static to the dynamic, from rigidity to "flexibility".

As a result, the spirit with which episcopal conferences should function is as important as the way in which they are structured. It is a spirit which has always in view the People of God, a body of human persons, by baptism made sons of God and of the Church, with all the rights of Christians, as well as all the rights of members of the Church.

Limits of Episcopal Conferences

The conferences will find in this fundamental conception of the human person as a member of the People of God a spontaneous limit to their normative activity. They will set their sights on the higher plan of the good of the community and will respect the internal autonomy of bishops which is prior to, and prevails over, specific collegial activity. They will reserve to the supreme authority of the Church that solicitude which, either by reason of its territorial competence, or, principally by reason of the very nature of the problems, lies outside the scope of an episcopal conference.

In this matter of balance, the episcopal conferences can find a luminous beacon in a consideration of the unity of the Church which is not simply a confederation of individual Churches. Each individual Church is the Church of Christ united in a concrete community. So also the union of bishops of several individual Churches always has a universal view of pastoral solicitude for the one Church of Christ even when a national or regional dimension would limit specific action. What matters is a positive union based on that radical and universal solicitude proclaimed by the Constitution on the Church when it treated episcopal collegiality.

Just as the activity of an episcopal conference is limited vertically, it meets with another limit on the horizontal level. This second demand on all authority in the Church involves the problem of the possibility of expediting *subordinate* internal autonomy, as much in physical as in moral persons, in the interior of the community, even when this autonomy is to coalesce with united pastoral action.

These demands place episcopal conferences in a state of per-

petual dynamism. At such times, it is good to avoid the tempta-
tion or the too hasty desire to crystallize structures on the supra-
diocesan level of the Church. We must be faithful to the function
of conferences which is to promote, according to the needs of
each moment, the life of the Church and, by the same token,
that of Christian and Catholic man in the diverse conditions of
his existence.

Multiple Functions of the Conference

The thing furthest from our intentions would be to conceive of
the conferences as being exclusively normative. Hence we must
at the very outset distinguish three aspects of episcopal conferences in their canonical role:

(a) decisions of legislative value which, were they to become
more permanent, could constitute the object of provincial or
plenary councils;

(b) decisions which, without becoming law in the proper sense,
are nevertheless juridically binding;

(c) pastoral or disciplinary agreements without strictly juridical binding force.

Conclusion

The Constitution on the Sacred Liturgy made use of a significant terminology in article 22 when speaking about competent
territorial authority. The *Motu Proprio Sacram liturgiam* determined for the time being that this authority would be constituted by national conferences of bishops. The provisional character of this ruling was again sanctioned in article 23 of the
Instruction of Sept. 26, 1964. The same *Instruction,* furthermore,
has admitted, in addition to national conferences, those of several
nations united together and legitimately constituted. It has opened
the door to the possibility of new proposals for episcopal group-
ings.

The plan of the conciliar decree refers specifically to national
or regional conferences. Nevertheless, this does not rule out ab-

solutely the possibility of episcopal conferences on various levels. The contrary is true, since the decree supposes that all dioceses will be grouped into ecclesiastical provinces, and these, in turn, when the time is right, into ecclesiastical regions. The same decree expressly speaks of territorial groups which would not be national.

The conferences must be legitimately constituted. We understand that in compliance with the letter and spirit of the intent of the Council's decree, conferences are constituted by the will of the bishops who form them, following the Council's exhortation which expressly states: *expedire censet*. The conference itself makes its own statutes. These are to be reviewed by the Holy See in the same way as is done in the actual proclamations of particular councils. It is not by chance that the same word *recognitio*, found also in canon 291, is used.

It is evident that the authority of the conference is ordinary. The Instruction *Inter oecumenici* in articles 25 to 31 contains specific norms for liturgical matters. For the rest, we believe it more opportune to postpone to a later article the study of concrete positive law which depends on the balloting of the fathers of the Council.

Joseph Hajjar/*Damascus, Syria*

The Synod
in the Eastern Church

s an institution, the synod represents the form of regional Church government in the Eastern Church. In this article the generic term "Eastern Church" is meant to cover the great Church that combines the various autocephalous branches of Byzantine origin and the minority Churches—Nestorian, Monophysite and the more recent Uniat Churches. In all these ecclesiastical groups the collegial activity of the bishops, gathered around their hierarchical head—whether patriarch, archbishop or catholicos—is the normal and even constitutional prerequisite for the more important decisions.

It is impossible to analyze in this brief survey all the manifestations and workings of this synodal activity. I shall have to limit myself to point out the many complementary forms and the essential, communal function which devolved upon the synod in the course of Church history. The ecumenical councils are not included here since they will be dealt with separately.

I

THE EARLY CENTURIES

All synodal activity in the Eastern Church is based on the example of the first Council of the Apostles in Jerusalem and has developed in that perspective. Hence this ecclesiastical tradition presents itself as the continuation and extension of the apostolic tradition. That is why the famous treatise, the *Synodicon* (the final draft of which goes back to the 10th century with several recensions still existing in manuscript) always begins the list of synods with that of Jerusalem. One of the most complete recensions, edited by Fabricius, counts up to 139 synodal assemblies of various kinds during the first ten centuries.[1]

It is true that up to the end of the 2nd century there was no synodal activity in the strict sense of the word but there was at least a certain extradiocesan solidarity among the bishops. This can be observed in Ignatius of Antioch, Polycarp of Smyrna and Denys of Corinth. But from that time on synods blossom forth in all the regions where Christianity has achieved a certain extension and some regional stability, as in Palestine, Rome, Pontus, Asia Minor, Osroene (or North Syria), Corinth and "in very many other regions", as Eusebius said.[2] The *synod,* then, constituted the institutional expression of the bishops' collegiality. Since then it has never ceased to be a typical feature of the Church's life and structure in the East. As the historical situation changed and ecclesiastical organization itself improved, this synodal institution acquired various external juridical forms.

Up to the first ecumenical Council of Nicaea the regional synod prevailed. Particularly in the East there were those of Palestine, Syria and Alexandria, in connection with the Easter question under Pope Victor (189-199). During the 3rd century there were others at Iconium and Synnades (about 230), several at Carthage (the first in 220, with seventy bishops), at Bostra in Syria (240 and 248), and at Antioch (260 and 268).[3] These early synods provided the later centuries with the first outline of a practice which gradually became an institution. That is why

[1] Fabricius, *Bibliotheca graeca* (ed. Harles), Vol. 12, pp. 358ff. "Libellus synodicon, omnes synodos, tam orthodoxas quam haereticas brevi commendio continens." (The *Synodicon,* containing short descriptions of all the orthodox as well as heretical synods.)

[2] Eusebius, *Ecclesiastical History* (Eng. trans. H. J. Lawlor and J. E. L. Oulton, London, S.P.C.K., 1927-8), V, pp. 23-5.

[3] J. Daniélou and Henri Marrou, *The Christian Centuries* (London: Darton, Longman and Todd, 1964), pp. 187ff.

their study is valuable for the historian and the canonist. I wish only to point out that they are not limited to the boundaries of civil or ecclesiastical provinces. The most representative members of the hierarchy in a region, in the broadest sense of the word, take part in them either in order to discuss and decide doctrinal issues or to take general or important disciplinary measures.

The provincial synod, in the strict sense, is well established and formally organized by the 4th century. In practice the ecclesiastical province is based on existing civil boundaries. From then on, the election, consecration and even the pastoral activity of the local bishop are dependent on the episcopal college of the province. The bishops of the same province hold their synod at certain clearly determined periods of the year under the presidency of the metropolitan or the bishop of the civil capital of the province. This metropolitan has a genuine authority of his own, but must make no final decisions without the general opinion of his suffragans. Canonical legislation, reinforced by that of Justinian (*Novella* 123, c.10; 137, c.4), laid down rules for this fundamental institution. The historical documents referring to it bear witness to its efficiency and continuity. This synodal institution has lasted practically up to our own days in the shape of the annual synods of the patriarchates and the autocephalous Churches. The metropolitan's presidency was not purely honorary; his guidance unquestionably maintained the agreement, harmony and unanimity among his provincial colleagues.

Apart from this provincial synod history shows two other kinds of synod which were, no doubt, of an incidental nature but had a considerable influence on the Church's destiny. First of all, there are a few councils, described in the sources of canon law as "topical", whose canonical legislation came to be universally accepted. Canon 2 of the Council *In Trullo* (692) which finally sanctioned the previous canonical sources, admitted them on the same basis as the ecumenical synods and the canons of certain Fathers of the Church. They are the synods of Ancyra, Neo-Caesarea, Sardica, Antioch, Gangres and Laodicea. Then there are the numerous councils held during the Arian crisis (325-380)

in the towns where the emperor or his court resided. Because of
the mobility of residence these genuine synods took place succes-
sively in Tyre, Jerusalem, Antioch, Sardica, Milan, Sirmium, Arles,
then again in Milan, Sirmium, and after that, simultaneously,
for the eastern and western sections of the hierarchy, at Seleucia
and Rimini, and then the list continues with Constantinople, Antioch, Sirmium and once again Constantinople. The bishops who
took part in these—one might say "imperial"—synods came from
every province of Christendom and were not necessarily court
prelates or courtiers. Imperial influence, whether accepted or
demanded, explains this peculiar phenomenon, which is not
limited to the East.

Above the provincial synod there were the synods of the great
patriarchal metropoles, rather limited in number, whose privileges
had been clearly fixed by the first four ecumenical councils. These
patriarchal Sees were those of Rome, Constantinople, Alexandria,
Antioch and Jerusalem. In Rome the famous Roman synods became prominent. In the other local primacies the patriarch consulted the metropolitans and archbishops of the various provinces
under his jurisdiction. But from 380 on, a special synod was
called together at Constantinople which the historical and canonical sources finally designated as *synodos endemousa* (in Latin:
synodus permanens) and which can be translated as "permanent
synod". The ecumenical Council of Chalcedon (451) officially
approved this kind of permanent synod in the presence of the
papal legates. This meant that whenever the seriousness of the
problems submitted to the authority of the Patriarch of Constantinople demanded it, he summoned the members of the hierarchy
present at that moment in the capital (*endemountes*) to a synod.
This synod then deliberated and took decisions under the presidency of the patriarch. The synod was permanent in the sense
that it could be convoked at any moment according to the seriousness of the situation, and because the Church considered herself
in a state of permanent synodal consultation while the members
of the hierarchy present, from the patriarch to the simplest bishop,
acted in solidarity for the common good. Since then this per-

manent synod became an official canonical institution of the college of bishops in the Byzantine Church. It exercised dogmatic vigilance, made legislative reforms and took disciplinary measures in a way that went beyond the traditional but limited role of the ordinary provincial synod, yet did not require the burdensome and always exceptional organization of an ecumenical synod.[4]

The provincial synod, like the patriarchal synod and the permanent synod of the patriarchate of Constantinople and of the Byzantine tradition, has remained the most representative and lasting forms of the collegial structure of the Eastern hierarchy. These institutions became more important and efficient with the centuries. Their status and competence are clearly determined by their own special rules. Yet, the synodal structure remained the basis of all major episcopal activity.

II

THE UNIAT CHURCHES OF THE EAST

History also throws light on the question whether the Eastern Churches, united with Rome, preserved this synodal character, under what conditions this synodal feature could operate and whether it did actually operate among the Uniats.[5]

Among the Churches that inherited the Byzantine tradition, practice varied according to the local situation and the amount of Roman influence on the inward development of each group.

The Ruthenians sealed their union with Rome at the Council of Brest-Litovsk in May, 1595. The following year Clement VIII himself determined the rights of the metropolitans responsible for that Church by the bull *Decet romanum Pontificem* of February 23, 1596. But a few decades later Urban VIII, in his bull *Sacrosanctum apostolatus officium* of March 12, 1625, laid down that a provincial synod be held every four years. The first took place

---

[4] J. Hajjar, *Le Synode Permanent (Synodos endemousa) dans l'Eglise byzantine des origines au XIe siècle* (Rome, 1962), esp. pp. 21-79.

[5] See C. de Clerc who finished Hefele-Leclerc's *Histoire des Conciles* with his double volume XI, which concerns these Uniat synods.

at Kolryn in 1626, the second not until 1720 (the famous synod of Zamosc),[6] and the third much later at Lwow in 1891.[7] These provincial synods were prepared either by Roman instructions or by commissions working in close collaboration with the Congregation of Propaganda under which the Uniat Churches had then been placed.

When the Rumanians were united with Rome they began by holding diocesan synods at Alba-Julia.[8] Their first truly provincial council took place only in 1872 at Blaj.[9] Previous legislation on important questions was in the hands of the Propaganda, as when in 1858 it issued three Instructions on clerical marriage, mixed marriages and the indissolubility of marriage. Even the provincial Council of Blaj had been prepared by appropriate *Instructions* from Rome. Two other provincial synods were held at Blaj in 1882[10] and 1900 respectively. The diocesan synods then promulgated the provincial decisions for each eparchy.

In the case of the Italian Greeks the Holy See itself legislated without intermediaries, as can be seen in Clement VIII's Instruction *Super aliquibus ritibus Graecorum* of August 31, 1595, and Benedict XIV's Letter *Etsi pastoralis* of March 6, 1743.[11]

The Melchites have always maintained that they looked after their own legislation in patriarchal synods and according to local needs. But the Propaganda has always reserved the right to approve these synods, rebuke them, or not recognize them at all. Thus the first synod of St. Sauveur (1736) was contested by Benedict XIV's Letter *Demandatam* of December 24, 1741,[12]

[6] *Collectio Lacensis (Acta et decreta sacrorum conciliorum recentiorum)*, II, pp. 1-74.

[7] *Acta et decreta synodi provincialis Ruthenorum Galiciae habitae Leopolis* (Rome, 1896).

[8] N. Nilles, *Symbolae ad illustrandam historiam Ecclesiae orientalis in terris coronae S. Stephani* (Innsbruck, 1885), pp. 162ff. These diocesan synods were relatively frequent, as in 1697, 1699, 1700-1701, 1702, 1703, 1707, 1711, etc.

[9] Mansi, *Amplissima collectio conciliorum*, XLII, pp. 463-616.

[10] *Idem.*, XLV, pp. 665-800. Note the corrections and changes added by the Propaganda to certain decisions taken by the members of the Rumanian hierarchy.

[11] *Coll. Lacensis*, II, pp. 448-50, and for *Etsi Pastoralis*, pp. 507-22.

[12] Mansi, *op. cit.*, XLIV, pp. 261-70 and 331-8.

which forbade any innovations in Byzantine discipline. After a few less important ones the synod of 1790 was prepared by a detailed Instruction sent out by the Propaganda.[13] But the synod of Karkafe (1806), held without any intervention by Rome, was rejected after many ups and downs.[14] Maximos III Mazloum held a synod in 1849 under the same conditions and experienced the same fate.[15] In the meantime the synod of Ain-Traz (1835) had been confirmed only *in forma communi* (in general) after many exchanges, explanations and confrontations.[16] Finally, at the insistence of Leo XIII and Pius X, and after being very carefully prepared by a mixed commission which met in Rome in 1901, the last patriarchal council took place at Ain-Traz in 1909 but was impeded by general indifference.

The same phenomenon can be observed in the other Eastern Churches. The synods are often carefully prepared in Rome or are held under the presidency of a papal legate with extensive powers. The Maronite synods of 1578, 1580 and 1596 were called and presided over by Jesuits acting as papal legates and applying their detailed instructions too literally.[17] Later the famous synod of Mount Lebanon of 1736 was drafted entirely and beforehand in Rome by the legate Joseph-Simon Assemani who imposed it on the episcopal gathering, not without difficulty and some intrigue.[18]

Under Pius IX the Propaganda decided to give non-Byzantine Uniat Churches a legislative system inspired by that of Trent. In this frame of mind the Jesuit Benoît Planchet, Pro-Apostolic Delegate of Mesopotamia, presided over the synod of the Chal-

[13] *Ibid.*, pp. 625-54.

[14] *Ibid.*, pp. 685-810 and 875-6. For this synod and the next, as for that of 1835, see J. Hajjar, *Un lutteur infatigable, le Patriarche Maximos III Mazloum* (Harissa, Lebanon, 1957), and W. de Vries, *Rom und die Patriarchate des Ostens* (Freiburg/Munich, 1963), esp. pp. 268ff.

[15] Mansi, *op. cit.*, XLIV, pp. 1019-1140.

[16] *Ibid.*, pp. 981-1020.

[17] See particularly G. Levenq, *La première mission de la Compagnie de Jésus en Syrie* (Beirut, 1925), pp. 3ff., and P. Dib, "Maronites," in *Dictionnaire de Théologie catholique*, cols. 60ff.

[18] C. de Clerc, *Histoire des conciles,* XI, Vol. 1, pp. 213ff. and P. Dib, *loc. cit.*, pp. 79ff.

dean Christians in 1852[19] and that of the Syrians in 1853-4.[20] The Acts of these two synods closely resemble each other and show a rather latinizing tendency. While the Chaldeans did not openly dare refuse a legislation imposed on them and later frequently ignored in practice, the Syrians hastened to recover their old liturgical customs at the synod of Aleppo in 1866. The Maronites held their synod at Bkerke in 1856 under the presidency of apostolic delegate Brunoni but he failed to persuade them to allow some Latin missionaries to take part as theologians.[21]

The preparatory Oriental commission of Vatican Council I made an effort to unify Oriental discipline, but did so by practically suppressing it altogether in favor of Latin uniformity. Toward the end of their labors they allowed one well-chosen Oriental delegate to take part. At the council itself, the Chaldean Patriarch Audo and the Melchite Patriarch Gregory Youssef reacted with clarity and courage. The Chaldean Patriarch maintained in particular that patriarchal or national synods were the most effective and traditional means of bringing about a religious and ecclesiastical reform. But the council did not have time to deal with the projects that had been prepared.[22]

It is true that Leo XIII inaugurated a period rich in initiatives leading to better understanding and collaboration with regard to the Christian East. But, insofar as the synods were concerned, there was no change in the demands of the Propaganda. It demanded as a guarantee that the synods be held under the presidency of a papal legate and other Latin theologians, and their

[19] Not wishing to mention the results of my own research on this subject in the archives of the Propaganda, I shall simply refer to articles that are easily accessible: Korolevsky, "Audo," in *Dict. Hist. Géogr. Eccl.*, cols. 324ff.; Tisserant, "Nestorienne (Eglise)," in *Dict. Théol. cath.*, XI, cols. 157ff.; Dauvillier, "Chaldéen (droit)," in *Dict. Théol. cath.*, II, cols. 2028ff. and C. de Clerc, whose already quoted work is fundamental for all this.

[20] P. Bacel, "Le premier synode syrien de Charfé," in *Echos d'Orient*, XIV (1911), pp. 293ff., based on acts of Arab synods sent to Rome to be examined. C. de Clerc, *op. cit.*, XI, Vol. 2, pp. 571ff.

[21] C. de Clerc, *op. cit.*, XI, Vol. 2, pp. 667ff.

[22] J. Hajjar, *Les chrétiens uniates du Proche-Orient* (Paris, 1962), pp. 292ff.

decisions could not be promulgated before Rome's approval had been obtained. It was under these conditions that a Syrian synod was held at Charfeh in 1888 and a Coptic synod at Cairo in 1898.[23]

The project for the issue of an Oriental Code of Canon Law, announced on January 5, 1929, finally removed the traditional power of legislation from the local synods. In fact, the successive publication of the various parts of this Code showed that the legislative unification of Oriental law became a *fait accompli* although patriarchal and local synods were left free to fill in certain details of the legislative system that had thus been unified. Nevertheless, the annual provincial synod has precisely the same status as the episcopal conferences in Latin law, without any proper deliberative and legislative power. The institution of the permanent synod re-introduced and universalized, has but a very limited administrative and judicial competence.[24]

Vatican Council II, particularly in its two Decrees on Ecumenism and on the Eastern Churches, shows a hopeful return to the Eastern tradition. The Decree on Ecumenism solemnly affirms the right to preserve the spirit, the liturgy, the theology and the spirituality proper to the East. The Decree on the Eastern Churches reaffirms their right to govern themselves according to their own norms and institutions. But it is only in the paragraph referring to the institution of the patriarchate that it is said that "the patriarchs constitute, together with their synods, the superior instrument (*instance supérieure*) of government". After reading those two decrees carefully, it seems to me that the institution of the synod, the keystone of the organic structure of the Eastern Churches, has been overshadowed by the affirmation of principles, however necessary, and by the emphasis placed on the patriarchate. Would it not have been better if more consideration and firmer expression had been given to the indispensable and

---

[23] *Ibid.*, esp. pp. 309-19 and C. de Clerc, *op. cit.*, XI, Vol. 2, pp. 599ff. and 759ff.

[24] *Acta Apostolicae Sedis, Motu Proprio: Sollicitudinem nostram,* entitled *De Judiciis pro Ecclesia Orientali,* (January 6, 1950) Can. 17-18 and 86-90.

central function of the synod in Eastern tradition and practice?
The place of the synod would then have been more clearly indicated in the way it deserves; for it remains inseparable from
the institution of the patriarchate which it conditions and justifies.
Above all, the proper character and safeguard of Church government in the East would have been better preserved on the same
grounds as the patriarchate.

Wilhelm de Vries, S.J./*Rome, Italy*

The "College of Patriarchs"

The college of bishops, headed by the pope as heir to St. Peter's office, is the successor of the college of the apostles. The first one thousand years, during which East and West were still organically united in the universal Church, and to which this article is confined, show that there was a certain classification within this body of bishops, particularly in the patriarchates. At the head of each patriarchate stands a bishop who embodies the fullness of episcopal power and in whose favor the other bishops have renounced part of their rights for the sake of better government in the Church.[1] The question is whether these higher bishops or patriarchs constitute by themselves a distinct "college", again under the leadership of Peter's successor, and whether this body is entitled to some supreme collegial authority over the whole Church. The answer is "no" if we mean by "college" a corporate body, such as a supreme Senate in the Church, which would meet regularly or at least rather frequently and which would have certain definite and canonically determined rights in the government of the universal Church. In fact, this situation has never existed, whether in Rome or in Constantinople. Even the *synodos endemousa* which played

---

[1] This seems to be the most plausible explanation of the rights of the patriarchs, as I have tried to show elsewehere; cf. W. de Vries, *Rom und die Patriarchate des Ostens* (Freiburg, 1963), pp. 7ff. The authority of the patriarchs originated through legal custom, sanctioned by the first councils. The implied consent of the pope as head of the universal Church must be taken for granted. During the first ten centuries even Rome did not look on the authority of the patriarchs as a share in the supreme authority of Peter's successor granted by the pope. It is linked rather with episcopal authority of which it represents the plenitude.

an important part in Constantinople in the government of the whole Eastern Church, did not, as we shall see, represent the patriarchate, nor was it a Senate of Patriarchs.

Nevertheless, the patriarchs form a unity, a whole, to which apostolic succession belongs in a very special way. This "whole" or "college" has decisive importance for the "communion" of all bishops among themselves and with their head, the successor of Peter, and a certain supreme collegial authority is attributed to it in ecumenical councils and other special functions. We can therefore rightly speak of "college of patriarchs" although not in a strict juridical sense. This college will, of course, look different according to whether we approach it from the point of view of Rome or from that of the East.

I

THE "COLLEGE OF PATRIARCHS" FROM THE POINT OF VIEW OF ROME

In reality Rome recognized only three patriarchal Sees as "units" in the strict sense of the word. They are the so-called Petrine Sees of Rome, Alexandria and Antioch, which are identified by their common apostolic, or even Petrine, origin. The popes had certain reservations about the claims of Constantinople and Jerusalem because these were based on the law laid down by the Council of Chalcedon which Leo the Great already considered contrary to the inspired and therefore inviolable Canon of Nicaea.[2] Nicholas I still recognized the bishops of Constantinople and Jerusalem as patriarchs in name only.[3] In practice, however, the popes recognized the patriarchates of Constantinople and Jerusalem, albeit reluctantly. In 591 Gregory the Great informed the patriarchs of Constantinople, Alexandria, Antioch and Jerusalem together of his election.[4] Here the order, usual in

[2] *Ibid.*, p. 354; cf. Leo, *Epistola* 104, n. 3; *P.L.* 54, col. 995.

[3] *Acta Romanorum Pontificum a S. Clemente I (c. 90) ad Coelestinum III* (died in 1198), I (Pont. Comm. ad redigendum Codicem Iuris Can. Or. Fontes, Series III, Vol. I) (Vatican, 1943), p. 679, n. 328 XCII; cf. *P.L.* 119, col. 1012.

[4] *Monumenta Germaniae Historica, Gregorii Papae Registrum Ep.* I, P. Ewald (Berlin, 1891) (*Mon. Ger. Hist. Gr. Reg.*), Liber I, n. 24, pp. 28f.

the East, is already accepted *de facto*. This order was incorporated in canon 21 of the fourth Council of Constantinople (869), and one can take it that Pope Hadrian II recognized this order when he officially approved the council's decisions.[5]

The popes, however, do not recognize a pentarchy of five patriarchs, as usually accepted in the East. In their view, only the three Sees which were derived from Peter had a real patriarchal function. The classic text clearly underlining the unity of the three Petrine Sees stands in the letter sent by Gregory the Great to Eulogius of Alexandria in November, 597:

"Although, then, there are many apostles, supreme authority belongs only to the See of the prince of apostles, and this See is one and the same (Peter's) though it exists in three places. For he himself enhanced the See where he entered upon his rest and ended his earthly life; he also honored the See to which he sent his disciple, the Evangelist (Mark), and he consolidated the See which he occupied for seven years although he left it afterward. Since, therefore, only one See is concerned, belonging to one person, but now occupied by three bishops by divine right, I count as mine all the good I hear of you; and when you hear something good about me, you must attribute it to your own merit because we are one in him who said, 'That all may be one, even as thou, Father, in me and I in thee, that they also may be one in us' " (John 17, 21).[6]

The point here is not to examine the historical and theological contents of this teaching about the three Petrine Sees, which was also held by such popes as Damasus, Leo the Great, Nicholas I and Leo IX,[7] but simply to state the fact that in the mind of these

[5] Letter of the Pope, Nov. 10, 871; cf. P. Jaffe and W. Wittenbach, *Regesta pontificum Romanorum ad a. p. Ch.* n. MCXCVIII (Leipzig, 1851); 2nd ed., 1881-1888 (Photomech, reprint, Graz, 1956), n. 2943; cf. *P.L.* 122, col. 1309; J. D. Mansi, *Sacrorum conciliorum nova et amplissima collectio*, 31 Vols. (Florence-Venice, 1757-1798) [New impr. and cont. ed. by L. Petit and J. B. Martin, 60 Vols. (Paris, 1899-1927)], Vol. 16, p. 206; for the canon of the Council, see Mansi, *op. cit.*, XVI, p. 174. Cf. A. Fliche and V. Martin, *Histoire de l'Eglise des origines jusqu'à nos jours* (Paris, 1937), Vol. 6, p. 489.

[6] *Acta Rom. Pont.*, 498, n. 268; cf. *Mon. Ger. Hist. Gr. Reg.*, VII/37, pp. 485-6.

[7] Cf. W. de Vries, *op. cit.*, pp. 351ff.; cf. also A. Michel, "Der Kampf

popes these three patriarchal Sees constituted a strict unity, with a special function in the government of the universal Church.

Rome felt that it was united to Alexandria and Antioch by a very special bond. Gregory the Great expressed this bond with Alexandria in a letter to Patriarch Eulogius as follows:

"As masters and disciples of this man (St. Peter) we are closely united so that I seem to rule over the See of the disciple because of the master, and you over the See of the master because of the disciple." [8]

The faith of the Church of Rome and that of Alexandria is of decisive importance for the whole Church. In his letter to John of Antioch and Juvenal of Jerusalem, in which he informed them of the excommunication of Nestorius, Pope Celestine I appealed in the first instance to the faith of both the Roman and Alexandrian Churches[9] shared by the whole Church. According to Leo the Great, in a letter to Proterius, Patriarch of Alexandria, the significance of the Alexandrian faith lies in that the Egyptians were instructed in the truth by Mark, Peter's disciple.[10]

A similar though even closer link existed between Rome and Antioch, where St. Peter worked before he went to Rome. The Church of Antioch is therefore a "sister" Church of Rome (*germana*), a "partner" (*consocia*), a "sharer" (*consors*) of the Roman See with a similar task. Innocent I wrote to Boniface the Presbyter:

"The Church of Antioch, which St. Peter honored before he came to Rome, is like a sister to the Roman Church which, therefore, cannot bear a prolonged estrangement." [11]

---

um das politische oder petrinische Prinzip der Kirchenführung," in *Das Konzil von Chalkedon. Geschichte und Gegenwart*, ed. by A. Grillmeier and H. Bacht, Vol. 2 (Würzburg, 1953), pp. 500ff. (Grillmeier-Bacht).

[8] In *Mon. Ger. Hist. Gr. Reg.*, VI/58, p. 432 (Letter of July, 596).

[9] *Acta Rom. Pont.*, 130, n. 50 (Letter of Aug. 10, 430); cf. *P.L. 50*, col. 469.

[10] *Ibid.*, 275, n. 132 (Letter of March 10, 454); cf. *P.L. 54*, col. 1075; see also *Acta Conc. Oec.*, ed. E. Schwarz, II/4, p. 84.

[11] Letter of the year 415 (*Acta Rom. Pont.*, 102, n. 35); cf. *P.L. 20*, col. 546.

To Bishop Maximus of Antioch Leo the Great pointed out that the apostle Peter proclaimed the same Gospel in Antioch and Rome, and exhorted him to watch over the purity of this teaching together with the Bishop of Rome: "It is therefore right that you should share the pastoral solicitude of the Apostolic See in this matter." [12] Leo IX assured Patriarch Peter of Antioch of Rome's special care: "In this the great mother, the primary See of Rome, will never and nowhere fail her beloved daughter, her partner even, if necessary." [13]

This communion of all patriarchs among themselves and of all with their head, the successor of Peter, is particularly evident at the election of a new patriarch who notifies Rome and his colleagues of his election and receives the ecclesiastical "communio" from Rome and the others. Thus the community of the college of bishops, the highest body of Church government, comes about through its highest members who are in direct communion with each other. The main function of the college of patriarchs is precisely to link all the bishops together who are linked thereby with the head and with each other through the juridical and sacramental bond of the "communio".

The meaning of the notification of the election to the Bishop of Rome and the significance of his reply is clearly expressed, for instance, in the letter of Pope Simplicius to Acacius of Constantinople. The pope was informed of the election of Calendion to the See of Constantinople. Upon this he introduced Bishop Calendion solemnly to the college of bishops: "We have received the letter which bears witness to your love. We therefore convey our thanks through our brother and co-bishop Anastasius, who has come from the aforementioned region, by letter. There remains only our duty to receive the priestly state of our brother and co-bishop Calendion in the bosom of the Apostolic See and in communion with us, and to accept the bishop of this noble

[12] Letter of the year 415 (*Acta Rom. Pont.*, 262, n. 125); cf. *P.L.* 54, col. 1042; *Acta Conc. Oec.*, II/4, p. 73.
[13] *Acta Rom. Pont.*, 770, n. 369 (date: 1052-53); cf. *P.L.* 143, cols. 770t.

city within the union of the college (of bishops) through the grace of Christ our God" (*collegii unione numeramus*).[14]

Leo the Great imparted his "communio" to Anatolius of Constantinople with the words: "For this is the virgin Church, spouse of one man, Christ, who cannot be led astray by any error. Thus the unity of our pure communion will be inviolable throughout the world" (*una nobis sit unius castae communionis integritas*). In this we embrace the communion of your love." [15]

A confession of faith is an essential part of all these notifications of a patriarchal election. They are usually styled *Litterae synodales* or *Inthronistica,* and regularly contain such a confession.[16] In the same way the popes usually informed the other patriarchs and included in this document a confession of faith.[17] The communion of the patriarchs with each other and with their head was therefore rooted in the unity of faith.

The other bishops are in communion with Rome and so with the universal Church through their patriarchs. *Only* the patriarchs notified Rome of their election and received a reply from the pope. This assured them of belonging to this communion but was not equivalent to either an appointment or a transmission of jurisdiction, as I have pointed out elsewhere.[18] That the other bishops are in communion with the head of the Church through their patriarchs is occasionally mentioned explicitly. Pope Damasus sent Paulinus of Antioch a confession of faith to be signed by his suffragan bishops, and he added: "We have sent you a confession

[14] Letter of July 15, 482 (*Acta Rom. Pont.,* 318, n. 163); cf. *P.L.* 58, col. 55.

[15] Letter of April 13, 451 (*Acta Rom. Pont.,* 229, n. 103); cf. *P.L.* 54, col. 913; *Acta. Conc. Oec.,* II/4, p. 39.

[16] For examples, see V. Grumel, *Les Regestes des Actes du Patriarcat de Constantinople* (Constantinople, 1932): Cyriac of Constantinople to Gregory the Great (A.D. 596), *op. cit.,* n. 273; Paul II of Constantinople to Pope Theodore (A.D. 642), *op. cit.,* n. 299; Nicephorus I to Leo III (A.D. 811), *op. cit.,* n. 328.

[17] *Ibid.,* n. 819.

[18] Cf. W. de Vries, "Die Entstehung der Patriarchate des Ostens und ihr Verhältnis zur päpstlichen Vollgewalt. Ein Beitrag zur Frage nach dem Verhältnis von Episkopat und Primat," in *Scholastik* 37 (1962), pp. 348f.

of faith; for you should not hesitate and when it is a matter of receiving into the Church caution should not lead to dilatoriness. This confession of faith is not so much destined for yourself since you are already associated with us in the communion of the same faith, but rather for those who, by signing (this confession) wish to be in communion with you, and through you, dear brother, with us." [19]

The schism started by Acacius was settled when John, the Patriarch of Constantinople, signed the confession of faith proposed by the pope and so was again received into communion with Rome. The pope simply accepted this as implying that John's suffragan bishops had renewed their communion with Rome through him. The pope exhorted him to help bring about the reunion of the Churches of Alexandria and Antioch with Rome.[20]

Hence in the eyes of Rome the main function of the college of patriarchs is to secure the communion of all the bishops with the center of the Church. On the other hand, Rome admits that the patriarchs together have, at least on occasion and in a certain measure, a collegial authority in the universal Church. Rome, too, accepts the importance of the patriarchs' participation in ecumenical councils in the matter of their universal validity, even though this idea is not so clearly expressed in the West as in the East. For example, Nicholas I, in a letter written in 865 to Emperor Michael, compared the Council of Nicaea (325) with the synod which deposed Patriarch Ignatius. The Council of Nicaea had this advantage over the synod that there were not only many bishops present from many regions, but that the patriarchs presided over it: "But it is also reported that the patriarchs presided over it," while there was not one patriarch present at the synod which deposed Ignatius.[21]

In connection with the "Three Chapters" controversy, Pope Pelagius I (556-561) attributed to the "Apostolic Sees" (by

[19] A.D. 375, *Acta Rom. Pont.*, 71-72, n. 15; cf. *P.L.* 13, col. 356.
[20] Letter of July 9, 514 (*Acta Rom. Pont.*, 413, n. 214); cf. *P.L.* 63, cols. 455f.
[21] *Ibid.*, 624, n. 322; cf. *P.L.* 119, col. 945.

which he doubtless meant above all Rome, Alexandria and
Antioch) the authority to decide doubts about the meaning of
a decision taken by a general council. In 559 he wrote to the
patrician Valerian: "But whenever there is a doubt among some
about a general council, all who care about the salvation of their
souls will spontaneously have recourse to the Apostolic *Sees* to
have explained what they have not understood." [22] On the same
point Gregory the Great appealed to the "Apostolic Sees" about
585 when he was still a deacon in the service of Pelagius II.[23]
According to Nicholas I a patriarch is confirmed in office, not
merely by the pope, but also by being received in communion
by all the other patriarchs. The pope was writing to Caesar Bardas
about Patriarch Ignatius who was unjustly removed from his
See. The Church of Constantinople had been entrusted to him
by God, and his election was "confirmed by the consent and
signature of all the priests of the provinces and by the *communio*
of his co-patriarchs".[24] John VIII appealed against Michael, King
of the Bulgarians, to the fact that the decision given by the Holy
See against Photius had been confirmed by all the patriarchs:
"Have your eyes not seen and your ears not heard that the judgment of the Holy See has been irrevocably accepted by all the
patriarchal Sees?" [25] After the rehabilitation of Photius the same
pope wrote to the Caesars Basil, Constantine and Alexander,
and referred again to the consent of the other patriarchs, this
time by name; the patriarchs of Alexandria, Antioch and Jeru-

[22] *P.L.* 69, col. 413 B.
[23] Cf. A. Michel (Grillmeier-Bacht), *op. cit.*, Vol. 2, p. 511 and footnote 94. The letter which Pelagius II sent to Elias of Aquileia and the
bishops of Istria and which was drafted by Gregory as the pope's deacon-
secretary, referred in his argument against the doctrine of Theodore of
Mopsuestia to Proclus of Constantinople, John of Antioch, Cyril of
Alexandria and a certain priest Hesychius who represented the patriarch
of that apostolic See. Cf. *Mon. Ger. Hist. Gr. Reg.* II, Appendix III/3,
pp. 459-60.
[24] Letter of Nov. 13, 866, (*Acta Rom. Pont.*, 658, n. 327); cf. *P.L.*
119, col. 1054.
[25] A.D. 873, in *Acta Rom. Pont.*, 711, n. 340; cf. *Mon. Ger. Hist. Gr.
Reg.* VII/2, 294, n. 312, App. Ep. 37.

salem.[26] In his eyes, therefore, their judgment carries great weight.

A letter written by Pope Agapitus to Patriarch Peter of Jerusalem in 536 points in the same direction. Agapitus reproached the patriarch for not having informed him about the nomination of the heretical Patriarch Anthimos to the See of Constantinople, and for having confirmed this nomination by his own consent.[27] So we see again that the consent given to the election of a patriarch by his colleagues is equivalent to a *confirmatio*, similar to that given by the Bishop of Rome.

On the other hand, there is no doubt that this Bishop of Rome considers himself head of the college of patriarchs. When he grants *communio*, this is unquestionably decisive. Whoever is received into this *communio*, belongs to the Church and is the legitimate patriarch; this cannot be said when this *communio* fails. Within the college of patriarchs the Bishop of Rome is not merely a *primus inter pares* (first among equals), but he holds a leading position that is decisive. This can be proved by numerous texts, too many for the scope of this article. I can give only a few instances.

Pope Leo IX, whose ghost-writer was the aggressive Cardinal Humbert of Silva Candida, uncompromisingly expressed the necessity of communion with Rome in a letter to Emperor Michael, of January 1054: "The Roman Church is so little alone, or as you seem to think, but one among many that any nation anywhere on earth which arrogantly breaks off relations with her, can no longer be called "Church" and considered as such, but is rather nothing at all or perhaps a false council of heretics or a gathering of schismatics and a synagogue of Satan." [28] This text presupposes of course, as is clear from the word *superbe* (arrogantly), that the here-mentioned schismatics and heretics act with malicious intent. An irenic attitude was still absent from the mentality of those days.

[26] Letter of Aug. 16, 879, (*Acta Rom. Pont.*, 723, n. 349); cf. *P.L.* 126, col. 854.

[27] Letter of March 13, 536, (*Acta Rom. Pont.*, 431, n. 227); cf. *P.L.* 66, col. 50.

[28] In *Acta Rom. Pont.* 781, n. 371; cf. *P.L.* 143, col. 776.

But long before this time the Holy See used to demand that anyone who wanted to be in communion with Rome should not be in communion with those to whom the successor of Peter refused this communion. An illustration of this is provided by the letter of Pope Felix III to Thalasios, an archimandrite in the city of Constantinople, whom the pope strictly forbade to get in touch with Acacius before Rome had granted him her *communio*.[29]

As true head of the college of patriarchs, the Bishop of Rome claimed the authority to decide against his colleagues if necessary. Thus, for instance, Pope Sergius rejected the Acta of the Trullan Synod (692), although they had been signed by three Eastern patriarchs.[30] Nicholas I referred to the case of the "Robbers' Council" of Ephesus, in 449, which was rejected by Rome although accepted by patriarchs.[31]

II

THE COLLEGE OF PATRIARCHS FROM THE POINT OF VIEW OF THE EAST

Lack of space allows only a very brief survey. I have been mainly concerned to show that Rome, too, recognized a certain collegiality of patriarchs. That this collegiality operated in the East has been known for a long time, and I shall refer only to some of the most important evidence.

The five patriarchs were compared in the East to the five senses of Christ's Mystical Body. Anastasius the librarian, who was really a Westerner but was trained by Greek monks in Rome, developed this point in his introductory speech at the fourth Council of Constantinople (869), which was essentially an Eastern council. In his Body, which is the Church, Christ has instituted five senses, just as any mortal body has five senses. These are the five patriarchs. The See of Rome is more in communion

[29] Letter of May 1, 490, (*Acta Rom. Pont.,* 347, n. 179); cf. *P.L.* 58, col. 975; cf. *Acta Rom. Pont.* 388, n. 192.

[30] *Acta Rom. Pont.,* 580, n. 306; cf. *Liber Pontificalis,* ed. L. Duchesne (Paris, 1886), Vol. 1, p. 373.

[31] *Acta Rom. Pont.,* 625, n. 322; cf. *P.L.* 119, col. 947.

with all than any other.[32] The five patriarchs therefore constitute a strict unity, a supreme government body, of which Rome is the head. They are closely linked together and must be concerned for each other. In the same way Theodore of Studios asked the other Eastern patriarchs to show some concern for the distress which beset the patriarchate of Constantinople (at the time of the iconoclastic controversy). It was their duty.[33] This courageous protagonist of the veneration of icons developed the theory of the pentarchy in a thoroughly orthodox manner. So much has already been written about this that I can be brief.[34]

According to Theodore the five patriarchs are in a very special way the successors of the apostles: the Bishop of Rome who occupies the first See, the second place belonging to Constantinople, and then the patriarchs of Alexandria, Antioch and Jerusalem following. "These are the five peaks of the Church's authority, and it is their judgment which must decide on divine dogmas."[35] The metropolitan Metrophanes of Smyrna declared at the fourth Council of Constantinople that God had established great luminaries on this earth (like the great luminaries in the sky), namely the five patriarchs, to enlighten the whole globe.[36]

According to the Easterns there are a number of cases where this college of five patriarchs has a definite collegial authority. With the exception of Rome each of these patriarchs can be judged by the other four if he deviates from the true faith or commits some other grave wrong. Thus the priest Elias, representing the Patriarch of Jerusalem at the fourth Council of Constantinople, declared that Photius had been condemned by Rome and the three other (patriarchal) Sees. The case had, therefore,

[32] Mansi, op. cit., XVI, p. 7.
[33] P.G. 99, cols. 1396 D–1397 A.
[34] For instance: S. Salaville, Studia Orientalia Liturgico-Theologica (Rome, 1940), pp. 228ff., "De 'Quinivertentia Ecclesiastico corpore' apud S. Theodorum Studitum"; M. Gordillo, Theologia Orientalium cum Latinorum comparata (Rome: Orientalia Christiana Analecta 158, 1960), pp. 122ff.; M. Jugie, Theologia dogmatica Christianorum Orientalium Vol. 4 (Paris, 1931), pp. 451ff.; R. Vancourt, "Patriarcats," in Dictionnaire de Théologie catholique XI, cols. 2269ff.
[35] In P.G. 99, col. 1417 (Epistolae, Vol. 2, n. 129).
[36] Mansi, op. cit., XVI, p. 82, Actio 6.

been decided. What had been decided in common by Rome and the other Sees was final.[37] Theodore of Studios wrote in a letter: "If one of the patriarchs errs he should accept correction by others of the same rank, as has been handed down to us by the great Dionysius." [38] In a letter to a monk called Anastasius, Maximus Confessor said that it was held against him that all the patriarchs (of Constantinople, Rome, Antioch, Alexandria and Jerusalem) were united in the matter of one will in Christ, and that he ought to submit to that judgment.[39] Photius wrote in 862 to the Armenian Catholicos Zacharias, whom he wanted to win over to union with the Byzantines, that it was absolutely impossible for all five patriarchs to err together.[40] Together, then, the five patriarchs would be infallible in matters of faith.

The ecumenical character of a council depends on whether all, or at least the majority of the patriarchs were represented. Patriarch Eutychius proved the complete validity of the second Council of Constantinople by the fact that four patriarchs were personally present: Vigilius of Rome, Eutychius of Constantinople, Apollinaris of Alexandria and Dominus of Jerusalem, "who, welded together as one body is constituted of four elements, were unanimous and in this harmony had joined hands".[41] In his inaugural discourse at the fourth Council of Constantinople Anastasius the librarian maintained that the synod had to be taken as ecumenical because all the patriarchal Sees were represented.[42] In his *Disputatio cum Pyrrho* Maximus Confessor held that the synod to which his correspondent appealed was not canonical since no "encyclical letter" had been issued by it with "the consent of the patriarchs".[43] Theodore of Studios also emphasizes that only a synod approved by the five patriarchs could be valid.[44]

I have already pointed out that the theory of the pentarchy,

---

[37] *Ibid.*, XVI, p. 35, Actio 1.
[38] In *P.G.* 99, col. 1419 (Ep. Vol. 2, n. 129, to Leo the "Sacellarius").
[39] *P.G.* 90, col. 132 A.
[40] V. Grumel, *op. cit.*, n. 473.
[41] In *P.G.* 86, col. 2308 BC.
[42] Mansi, *op. cit.*, XVI, p. 7.
[43] In *P.G.* 91, col. 352.
[44] *P.G.* 99, col. 1306, Ep. Vol. 2, n. 72; cf. *ibid.*, col. 1420 A, n. 129.

as held by the Greeks while they were still in communion with Rome (and also held by Anastasius the librarian who was secretary to Pope Nicholas I), in no way excluded the primacy. It is true that later on this theory developed in the sense of complete equality of all the patriarchs, including Rome, away from the primacy. I cannot deal in the brief space of this article with the complicated question in what sense the Greek Church held the primacy of the pope during the first millenium. I can refer to only one or two instances to show that this teaching was in any case accepted somehow. In fact, however, the Eastern patriarchates of Alexandria, Antioch and Jerusalem gravitated around Constantinople rather than Rome.

For Theodore of Studios Rome is the first See, to which one turns in cases of conflict, as in the matter of the veneration of icons, and where one looks for certainty in matters of faith.[45] The same Theodore admits that, according to ancient custom, orthodox synods cannot be convoked without informing the pope.[46] Canon 21 of the fourth Council of Constantinople expresses quite clearly the preeminence of Rome.[47] Many Easterns address the Bishop of Rome in their letters as "Universal Patriarch".[48] The papal primacy is fully recognized in a letter of the "highest priests of the East", *i.e.*, the patriarchs of Antioch, Jerusalem and Alexandria, to Tarasius of Constantinople, in which they explain that the Arab occupation prevents them from being present at the forthcoming synod of Constantinople. If necessary the synod could proceed without them, since this had also happened at the sixth synod (third Council of Constantinople, 680), which in spite of absences had rightly proclaimed the doctrine of the faith,

[45] *P.G.* 99, col. 1419, Ep. Vol. 2, n. 129.

[46] *Acta Rom. Pont.*, 923, n. 35 App.; cf. *P.G.* 99, cols. 1018f.

[47] Mansi, *op. cit.*, XVI, p. 171: "Furthermore, if a universal synod should be convened, and discuss with fitting respect the question at hand, and, fixing upon a solution, bring the discussion to a conclusion, still we would not be so arrogant as to condemn the supreme pontiffs of the preeminent Roman See."

[48] Thus Bishop Stephen of Larissa in a letter of Dec. 7, 531, (*Acta Rom. Pont.*, 891, n. 28 App.). Gregory the Great refused the title, as is known; cf. W. de Vries, *op. cit.*, p. 369; cf. *Acta Rom. Pont.*, 501, n. 271 and 913, n. 33 App.

the more so as the most holy and apostolic Pope of Rome had agreed and had been represented by his envoys.[49]

Yet, as has been said, for the Eastern patriarchates the most important center was, in fact, not Rome but Constantinople. The notification of patriarchal elections was much more frequently addressed to this center than to Rome, although even the exchange of information with Constantinople was not regular throughout because it was frequently prevented by adverse political situations. We still have, by way of illustration, the letter of Patriarch Tarasius of Constantinople (785) to the patriarchs of Alexandria, Antioch and Jerusalem. He asked them to support him as fathers in his lack of courage with the power of their episcopal staff and their fatherly teaching, and to help him as brothers. "According to holy and apostolic custom" he sent them a confession of faith to convince them of his orthodoxy.[50]

The Eastern patriarchs were represented by envoys in Constantinople if the political situation allowed. There is evidence for this already in the 6th century.[51] The name of the Patriarch of Constantinople was mentioned in the liturgy.[52] Since Chalcedon (451) Constantinople began to exercise a definite influence on these patriarchates. Even before that time many interventions have been recorded. Before 451 Anatolius of Constantinople ordained a bishop for Antioch, contrary to the canons.[53] Canons 9 and 17 of Chalcedon were interpreted, perhaps from the start, but certainly later on, as implying a right of appeal to Constantinople, also from other Eastern patriarchates.[54] E. Herman has

[49] *P.G.* 98, col. 1476.

[50] *Ibid.*, col. 1461.

[51] Cf. J. Pargoire, "Apocrisiaire," in *Dictionnaire de Théologie catholique*, I, cols. 2541f.

[52] V. Grumel, *op. cit.*, p. 787. This follows, for instance, from a letter of Patriarch Theophylact to the Eastern patriarchs, written in 937 or 938. This also shows that the use had been discontinued for centuries because of the political situation.

[53] Cf. J. Hajjar, *Le Synode Permanent dans l'Eglise Byzantine des origines au XIe siècle.* (Rome: Orientalia Christiana Analecta 164, 1962), p. 75; cf. *Acta Rom. Pont.*, 251, n. 119; *P.L.* 54, col. 1001.

[54] Hajjar, *op. cit.*, p. 45.

shown in detail how the primacy of Constantinople developed after the Council of Chalcedon.[55]

A decisive factor in this was the so-called *synodos endemousa*. It was composed of bishops who were resident in Constantinople or happened to be there at the time. Only now and then were bishops from the Eastern patriarchates or even patriarchs themselves present.[56] The *synodos endemousa* became a powerful instrument of centralization throughout the East. Through it Constantinople exercised its function of "ecumenical patriarchate" the authority of which extended beyond the boundaries of its own territory into that of the other patriarchates. According to J. Hajjar the disciplinary measures of the synod were limited to the Patriarchate of Constantinople, while the dogmatic decisions had an ecumenical bearing.[57] From the beginning of the 9th century the *synodos endemousa* took on also administrative functions in the general movement toward centralization which spread throughout Christendom,[58] and these extended beyond the territory of Constantinople.[59] Thus the synod became more and more an organ of central government for the whole Eastern Church, but it never became a kind of Senate of patriarchs.

Constantinople, then, was the center for the three Eastern patriarchates. Nevertheless, this did not mean that, apart from unfortunately frequent tensions, Rome's dominant leadership was put aside during these ten centuries. In 1024 Patriarch Eusta-

[55] Grillmeier-Bacht, *op. cit.*, n. 7, Vol. 2, pp. 459–90.

[56] At the synod of Constantinople, held under Bishop Nectar (381–397), Theophilus of Alexandria and Flavian of Antioch were also present; cf. Hajjar, *op. cit.*, p. 57; V. Grumel, *op. cit.*, Vol. 1, 1, 6; Mansi, *op. cit.*, III, p. 582. Maximus Confessor was condemned in 655 by the synodos endemousa in the presence of the Patriarch of Antioch and a representative of Alexandria; cf. Hajjar, *op. cit.*, p. 201; Mansi, *op. cit.*, XI, p. 357. Usually, however, only bishops belonging to the Patriarchate of Constantinople were members of this permanent synod. The synod can therefore not be taken as a permanent representation of the Eastern patriarchs in Constantinople. A list of the bishops present is given by J. Oudot, *Patriarchatus Constantinopolitani Acta Selecta* I (Codif. Can. Or. Font., II–III, Vatican, 1941), p. 181, n. 3; cf. Mansi, *op. cit.*, VIII, pp. 1047f.

[57] Hajjar, *op. cit.*, p. 191.

[58] *Ibid.*, p. 192.

[59] *Ibid.*, pp. 198f.

thius still sent a message to Pope John XIX, with gifts, to request that Rome recognize the Church of Constantinople as universal within its limits while Constantinople was prepared to recognize the preeminence of the Church of Rome throughout the world.[60]

Finally a brief word about what the Syrians who were separated from Rome, thought about the college of patriarchs.[61] The Syrian Monophysites recognized four patriarchs—those of Rome, Alexandria, Constantinople and Antioch, which were all instituted by apostles. If a patriarch erred in matters of faith "the other three should meet and judge him".[62] Of these four, two (Rome and Constantinople) had fallen away from the true faith. The Church is therefore limited to the patriarchates of Alexandria and Antioch.[63]

Among the Nestorians, the theory of the pentarchy is very similar to that of the Greeks. The five patriarchates are: one in the East, that of Seleucia-Ctesiphon, and four in the West, those of Rome, Alexandria, Antioch and Constantinople.[64] About this Timothy I (728–823) wrote: "One and the same Spirit perfects the Catholic Church which exists in all the heavenly regions, through these five Sees as through the five senses of body and soul...".[65]

We are therefore entitled to speak of a "College of Patriarchs," though not, as above, in the strict juridical sense of the words. In the East the idea of the collegial authority of the patriarchs was strongly developed, but in Rome, too, it was not unknown. There are, however, between Rome and the East many differences in detail and emphasis.

[60] Grumel, *op. cit.*, n. 828.

[61] Cf. W. de Vries, *Der Kirchenbegriff der von Rom getrennter Syrer* (Rome: Orientalia Christiana Analecta 145, 1955), pp. 7–12 and 45–7.

[62] *Ibid.*, p. 10; cf. J. B. Chabot, *Chronique de Michel, Patriarche Jacobite d'Antioche* (Paris, 1900–1910), Vol. 3, p. 68 and Vol. 2, p. 414.

[63] *Ibid.*, p. 11.

[64] *Ibid.*, p. 46.

[65] *Ibid.*, p. 46; cf. O. Braun, *Timothei Patriarchae I Epistolae* (Rome, 1915), pp. 101–2.

Willy Onclin/*Louvain, Belgium*

Collegiality and the Individual Bishop

The collegiality of the bishops is direct and formal only when they act as a college, that is, when all the bishops act together; this remains true whether they are together in an ecumenical council or dispersed throughout the world. The united action of the bishops as a body is directly concerned with the universal Church. It is the exercise of the full and supreme authority with which the college of bishops is endowed under the authority of the pope in the universal Church. The Constitution on the Church describes the fact as follows: "The supreme power in the whole Church, which this college enjoys, is exercised in a solemn way in an ecumenical council. A council is never ecumenical unless it is confirmed or at least accepted as such by the successor of Peter; and it is the prerogative of the Roman pontiff to convoke these councils, to preside over them and to confirm them. This same collegiate power can be exercised together with the pope by the bishops living in all parts of the world, provided that the head of the college calls them to collegiate action, or at least approves of or freely accepts the united action of the scattered bishops, so that it is thereby made a collegiate act." [1]

The college of bishops, then, exercises collegiate activity with

[1] *The Constitution on the Church* (Glen Rock, N. J.: Paulist Press, 1965), Arts. 22 ff.

regard to the universal Church principally, and in solemn fashion, in an ecumenical Council duly summoned or at least approved by the supreme pontiff. Scattered throughout the world, the bishops also exercise collegiate activity whenever (1) a point of doctrine is proposed or proclaimed with the consent of all the bishops or (2) a disciplinary measure which concerns the whole Church is promulgated with their assent or at the suggestion of a majority of bishops.

Nothing prevents the supreme pontiff from seeking the agreement of the bishops, by word of mouth or in writing, before proposing or defining a point of doctrine or deciding on some general disciplinary measure. In the same way, there is nothing to prevent the pope from approving or accepting a doctrine which the majority of bishops wish to see defined, or from confirming and promulgating a law which the majority of bishops consider necessary and want to see introduced into the universal Church. In these cases one can speak of direct and collective action by the college of bishops, as long as papal approval includes the intention to make this doctrinal or legislative action truly collegiate.

But these are not the sole manifestations of the collegiate activity of the bishops. This activity, indeed, is not exclusively limited to the exercise of the magisterium or of jurisdiction when issuing from the college as a whole. It is present all the time, at least in a concealed or habitual manner, and as such is somehow expressed in the preoccupations and juridical obligations of the bishop as a member of the college of bishops.

Indirectly, therefore, this episcopal collegiality is expressed in certain actions which do not emanate from the college as such, but from individual bishops or groups of bishops in the service of various particular Churches. It is certainly manifest in any action which directly concerns a particular Church but reflects the bishop's responsibility in relation to the universal Church. It is equally present in any action which conveys a bishop's preoccupation with individual Churches other than his own, and especially in any collective action taken by several bishops with

regard to a group of particular Churches in an ecclesiastical
province, a region, a nation or even a wider group.

Bishop's Responsibility with regard to the Universal Church

First of all, this collegiality shows in the numerous episcopal
activities which directly concern their own Church but are related
to the universal Church whose unity they aim to consolidate.

No doubt, the jurisdiction and magisterium of each bishop is
limited to the particular Church with which he has been entrusted.
Of this Church he is the rightful, ordinary and immediate shepherd, and he exercises his pastoral function from day to day, not
in the name of the pope but in the name of Christ himself. This
is formally stated in canon law (Can. 329, § 1; 334, § 1; 1327,
§ 1) and in the *Motu Proprio*: *Cleri sanctitati* (Can. 392, § 1;
397, § 1), and is confirmed by the Constitution on the Church.[2]
But while he is the rightful and ordinary shepherd of his own
flock, he cannot claim such authority over other Churches nor
over the Church as a whole. As the same Constitution puts it:
"The individual bishops, who are placed in charge of particular
Churches, exercise their pastoral government over the portion of
the People of God committed to their care, and not over other
Churches nor over the universal Church." [3]

On the other hand, a bishop heads some particular Church
only because he is in communion with the rest of the bishops
with whom he constitutes the college of bishops, and with the
head of this college, the pope. It is as a member of this college
and in communion with the pope that a bishop is put in charge
of a particular Church,[4] for such a Church cannot exist without

---

[2] *Ibid.*, Arts. 20, 27; cf. also 24, 33.

[3] *Ibid.*, Arts. 23, 27.

[4] Some authors, as recently as M. Kaiser, "Das Prinzip der Subsid-
iarität in der Verfassung der Kirche," in *Archiv für Kath. kirchenrecht*
133 (1964), p. 12, state that the bishops are primarily heads of particular
Churches and only as such exercise authority in the universal Church.
This seems inaccurate to me because, on the contrary, the bishops are
legitimate heads of the particular Churches only as members of the college
of bishops and in communion with this college and its head.

the bond uniting it to the universal Church which becomes a reality in the particular Church. From its earliest days the Church of Christ has taken shape in a multitude of communities, the particular Churches, which are all entitled to the name "Church" precisely because they carry into effect God's design in his Church. These individual Churches are therefore not autonomous Churches, but they are all united with one another and "in and from them comes into being the one and only Catholic Church" (Const. on the Church, Art. 23).

Since each bishop represents such an individual Church in which he has to "build up" the Church of Christ, he is bound to be the principle of unity linking his particular Church with the universal Church and to govern this particular Church in such a way as to promote the life of the Church as a whole. While being at the head of his individual Church, he is at the same time a member of the episcopal college, and as such responsible for the whole Church, whose unity of faith and discipline he must foster. He must therefore be concerned and feel himself responsible for that universal Church in whose life he must take part with the pope and the episcopal college to which he belongs.[5] The Constitution expresses this obligation of the bishops as follows: "It is the duty of all bishops to promote and to safeguard the unity of faith and the discipline common to the whole Church, to instruct the faithful to love the whole Mystical Body of Christ, especially its poor and sorrowing members and those who are suffering persecution for justice's sake." [6]

This obligation of the bishops to maintain the unity of faith and to watch over the unity of Church discipline is moreover laid down in the current law of the Church. Canon 1326 of the Code declares that although as individual bishops or grouped in local councils they are not infallible in their teaching, they are nevertheless the real doctors and teachers of the faithful who are entrusted to their care. According to Can. 1327, § 1, the bishops

---

[5] Cf. P. Parente, "La doctrine du Concile sur l'Eglise," in *La Documentation catholique* 62 (1965), p. 423.

[6] *Loc. cit.*, Arts. 23, 27–8.

have the duty to preach the Catholic faith; and paragraph 2 of the same canon commands that in principle they must themselves discharge this duty. They must give this instruction in the teaching of the Gospel first of all to the faithful because they must do all they can to preserve purity of faith and morals among the clergy and the Christian people, particularly among the less educated; they must also see to it that small children and young people are educated according to the principles of the Catholic religion.

But they also have this duty toward non-Catholic Christians and non-baptized persons, over whom they have no authority whatever. Hence Can. 1350, § 1, recommends to their care the non-Catholic Christians and unbelievers who live in their diocese and to whom they will try to bring the light of the Gospel. For, as the Constitution says: "The task of proclaiming the Gospel everywhere on earth pertains to the body of shepherds, to all of whom in common Christ gave his command, thereby imposing upon them a common duty, as Pope Celestine in his time recommended to the fathers of the Council of Ephesus." [7]

The Council of Trent also declared that preaching was the principal duty of the bishops.[8] And in his encyclical *Humani generis* Pope Benedict XV referred to this Council and said that the apostles, whose successors the bishops are, considered this their main task; he quoted St. Paul on this point: "For Christ did not send me to baptize but to preach the Gospel" (1 Cor. 1, 17).[9]

It follows also from the Constitution that the bishops act in a collegiate capacity when they maintain and promote the discipline of the whole Church. On this point, too, current canon law is not less formal. According to canons 336, §§ 1 and 2, of the Code and canon 400, §§ 2 and 3, of the *Motu Proprio: Cleri sanctitati* bishops must see to it that the laws of the Church are observed and that no abuses creep into ecclesiastical discipline.

By doing their duty with regard to the general discipline of the

[7] *Ibid.*, Arts. 23, 29.

[8] Council of Trent, *Decree on reformation*, session V, n. 9; session XXIV, Can. 4.

[9] Benedict XV, encyclical letter: *Humani generis*, Art. 6, in *AAS* 9 (1917), p. 307.

whole Church and the preaching of the Gospel the bishops will be, within their own Church, the bond that unites this Church with the other individual Churches and hence with the universal Church for which they are responsible as a college.

The Bishop's Responsibility for Churches Other than His Own

The bishops' collegiality shows no less in their responsibility for Churches other than their own. As members of the episcopal college which succeeded the apostolic college they have a general responsibility toward the universal Church, and hence toward all the individual Churches of which it consists. Here their duty will be more urgent toward those individual Churches that are in need or that are nearer to them. Hence the Constitution declares: "With all their energy, therefore, they must supply to the missions both workers for the harvest and also spiritual and material aid, both directly and on their own account, as well as by arousing the ardent cooperation of the faithful. And finally, the bishops, in a universal fellowship of charity, should gladly extend their fraternal aid to other Churches, especially to neighboring and more needy dioceses in accordance with the venerable example of antiquity." [10] Aware of this collegiate duty, bishops usually do their best to promote vocations for the missions and to rouse the generosity of the faithful in support of mission Churches; particularly in recent years many bishops have urged their priests to put themselves at the disposal of bishops in Latin America and other regions, where lack of priests has been the main cause of a decline in the faith and religious practice. It is moreover likely that future legislation, the principles of which will be laid down by the conciliar decree concerning the bishops, will bring greater elasticity to the rules now governing the matter of incardination and excardination of clergy in the dioceses.

Joint Episcopal Activity

The care for Churches other than their own, particularly for neighboring Churches, shows in the various ways in which bishops

[10] *Loc. cit.*, Arts. 23, 28.

collaborate on a juridical basis within the limits of a patriarchate, ecclesiastical province, or an even larger group. Up till now this joint activity of individual bishops has been organized by means of local councils which current canonical legislation has endowed with rather extensive powers. From now on this activity will apparently be strengthened by episcopal conferences.

The local councils recognized by Latin canon law are (1) the provincial council, which must be held at least every twenty years in every ecclesiastical province (Can. 283), and (2) the plenary council, where the ordinaries of several ecclesiastical provinces meet, usually on a national basis. Such a national council can be held only with the approval of the pope whose legate convokes and presides over such a council (Can. 281). Similar regulations exist in the legislation for the Eastern Churches, contained in the *Motu Proprio*: *Cleri sanctitati*. These regulations assert that a patriarchal, archiepiscopal or provincial synod must be held whenever the patriarch or archbishop (with the agreement of the permanent synod) or the metropolitan (with the consent of the bishops of the province) judges it necessary, and in any case at least once in twenty years (Can. 344); an "inter-ritual" synod of bishops belonging to different rites, and an interprovincial synod of bishops belonging to provinces other than those under the jurisdiction of the patriarch or archbishop, may also be held with the approval of the pope (who will appoint a legate to convoke and preside over such a synod).

These synods and local councils have very wide powers since they can examine and lay down any measures for their respective territories which may strengthen faith and morals, correct abuses, settle controversies and maintain or restore unity of discipline (Can. 290, and *Motu Proprio: Cleri sanctitati*, Can. 349). Yet, because these synods and councils are difficult to organize and demand a long preparation, one may say that they do not really and adequately encourage collaboration between bishops of the same province, and particularly not between bishops of a whole nation. Closer and easier collaboration between bishops on a regional or national level has now been made possible by the regional or national episcopal conferences, the principles of which will be established by Vatican Council II.

These episcopal conferences are not entirely new. Current legislation in both East and West provides for episcopal conferences, but these are only provincial ones (for bishops within one province). They must be held at least every five years according to Latin canon law (Can. 292, § 1), and at least once a year according to Oriental canon law (*Motu Proprio: Cleri sanctitati,* Can. 351, § 1). But these conferences have no power to make decisions or to legislate; they can only deliberate on what ought to be done in the various dioceses of the province in order to foster religion and to prepare the work of the next provincial council. It naturally provides the bishops with an opportunity to (1) agree on what line to take and (2) to carry out, each in his own diocese, certain measures that have been agreed upon. But insofar as the faithful are concerned, such measures have only the authority of decisions made by the bishop of the diocese, not that of decisions of episcopal conferences. Regional, national or supra-national conferences are not provided for by present canon law, at least not explicitly. Nevertheless, canon 292, § 1 of the Code, which deals with provincial episcopal conferences, asserts that the Holy See may go against these measures in particular cases. It was in fact a decision of the Holy See which introduced regional conferences in Italy: they were set up by a decree of the Sacred Consistory, of March 24, 1919, and confirmed by a decree of the same Congregation of June 21, 1932.

Moreover, in many countries the hierarchy has in fact held national conferences, and this movement has been encouraged by Rome. Several of these conferences have laid down statutes later approved by Rome. There exists even a supra-national conference, the CELAM. (Consiglio Episcopale Latino-Americano), approved by Pius XII on November 2, 1955. But at present there is no general legislation dealing with these conferences and, at least until the promulgation of the liturgical decree of Vatican Council II, they possessed no legislative power. This decree in fact recognizes that these territorial conferences have a certain legislative competence, and the *Motu Proprio: Sacram liturgiam* of January 5, 1964, attributes this competence to national episcopal conferences.[11] It is in any case more than likely that the decree *De pastorali Episcoporum munere* will not only establish such national episcopal conferences but also endow them with some limited legislative competence.

There seems to me to be little doubt about the nature of the bishops' authority in these local councils and episcopal conferences. In both types of assembly the bishops exercise their episcopal authority in matters which belong to the magisterium and jurisdiction, *i.e.*, the authority which they rightfully exercise with regard to the Church which they govern under that Church's supreme authority, namely, the pope and the college of bishops. This supreme power not only directs and controls the use of episcopal authority but can also limit its exercise when the good of the universal, or even the particular Church, requires it.

In principle and as a general rule the exercise of this authority is individual, each bishop exercising it only in the particular Church of which he is in charge. But sometimes, namely, when the supreme authority of the Church deems it necessary to lay down a uniform regulation for the various dioceses of the same ecclesiastical province, region or nation, the exercise of this episcopal authority will be collective, so that the various bishops of a province, region or nation exercise their authority jointly for all the dioceses concerned. This is exactly the case in patriarchal synods, provincial and national councils, as well as in the episcopal conferences which, therefore, are but a new way of exercising collectively the authority each bishop has in his own diocese.

Consequently, when the bishops meet in local councils or episcopal conferences, they do not exercise their authority there by favor of the Holy See, which they do not represent, but by virtue of the episcopal authority which is strictly theirs. No doubt, the

---

[11] *Constitution on the Sacred Liturgy* (Glen Rock, N. J.: Paulist Press, 1964), Arts. 22b, 36c, 39–40, 44. Cf. also the *Motu Proprio* in the same edition of the Constitution, Art. 10 *(Sacram liturgiam)*.

decrees of the local councils cannot be promulgated until they have been *expensa et recognita* by the Holy See (Can. 291, §1, and *Motu Proprio: Cleri sanctitati*, Can. 350, § 1) but the *expensio et recognitio* mean only that these decrees must be submitted to and acknowledged by the Holy See,[12] and do not need a specific positive approval: they do not affect their juridical character. This recognition does not turn these decrees into decisions of the Holy See, but they remain measures taken by the bishops exercising jointly the episcopal authority that is theirs in the particular Churches over which they are placed.

It is true that plenary councils are convoked and presided over by a papal legate, but the reason for this is that there is no competent ecclesiastical authority between the pope and the metropolitans, so that when such an authority is required it must be requested of the pope.[13] The bishops' authority in these local councils is therefore not a delegated authority but an ordinary authority—the episcopal authority that is theirs. The same holds good for the authority to make decisions which the bishops exercise collectively in episcopal conferences.

According to the Constitution on the liturgy and the *Motu Proprio: Sacram liturgiam*, the measures that national episcopal conferences are competent to enact in matters liturgical must be submitted to the Holy See for approval or confirmation, *probanda seu confirmanda*.[14] As the text shows, however, this approbation is but a confirmation that does not affect the nature of these measures: though confirmed, they keep the juridical character they had before confirmation, and therefore remain episcopal decisions.

On the other hand, when bishops meet in local councils or episcopal conferences they are not simply representatives of the college of bishops either. The authority they exercise there is not what they have collectively with regard to the universal Church as united in the one college of bishops, but what they have as heads

[12] Cf. R. Naz, *Traité de droit canonique* I (Paris, 1954), nn. 587, 420.
[13] *Ibid.*, nn. 580, 417.
[14] *Constitution on the Sacred Liturgy* (Glen Rock, N. J.: Paulist Press, 1964), Art. 36c; *Motu Proprio: Sacram liturgiam* (Glen Rock, N. J.: Paulist Press, 1964), Art. 9.

of their own particular Churches. Hence the decrees of local councils and the decisions of episcopal conferences are not acts emanating from the college of bishops, directly or indirectly, but measures taken by bishops exercising collectively the authority they have in their own Churches.

Yet, the bishops' duty to make collective use of their individual episcopal authority in order to ensure the common good of a group of particular Churches implies that they are responsible for particular Churches other than their own and for the government of these Churches. Local councils and episcopal conferences may therefore be considered the juridical expression of the bishops' responsibility as members of the college of bishops and of their concern for all the Churches. As such they are a manifestation of episcopal collegiality.

PART II

BIBLIOGRAPHICAL SURVEY

Petrus Huizing/*Heverlee-Louvain, Belgium*

The Reform of Canon Law

1

PAPAL INITIATIVES

In his allocution *Questa festiva ricorrenza* of January 25, 1959, Pope John XXIII announced the synod of Rome and the Ecumenical Council which would lead to an *aggiornamento* of the *Codex juris canonici*, the legal Code in force in the Latin Church. This "updating" of the law would accompany and crown the work done by these two assemblies. It would be preceded by the promulgation of a Code for the Oriental Churches.[1] This "adjustment" of the Latin Code soon proved to require a complete renewal of ecclesiastical law,[2] the more so as it had to deal first of all with the executions of the decisions and directives laid down by the Council.[3] This situation remained the same under Pope Paul VI.[4]

[1] *Acta Apostolicae Sedis (AAS)* 51 (1959), pp. 68f.

[2] Encyclical *Ad Petri Cathedram*, of June 29, 1959, in *AAS* 51 (1959), p. 498: "We intend . . . to prepare a Codex of canon law adapted to the needs of today, and to publish a similar Codex for the Church of the Oriental rite . . ."; allocution to the cardinals on May 30, 1960, in *AAS* 52 (1960), p. 89: ". . . to update the Codex of canon law according to the demands of the present times . . ."; the Apostolic Constitution *Sollicitudo omnium ecclesiarum* of June 29, 1960, in *AAS* 52 (1960), pp. 551f.: ". . . to compose a book of Church laws to suit the needs our days . . ."; the complete documentation is given by U. Navarrete in *Periodica de re morali canonica liturgica* 49 (1960), pp. 139–41 and 50 (1961), pp. 134f.

[3] Cf. footnote 5.

[4] The day after his election Paul VI declared that he intended to con-

95

On March 28, 1963, two months before his death, Pope John announced the establishment of a commission for the revision of the Code. It would be unable to begin work until after the Council, but it could already contact conciliar commissions on topics left out of the schemata which were drastically curtailed after the first session; during the second session they could discuss their eventual suggestions with all the bishops.[5] On November 7, Paul VI added twelve members to the commission.[6] On April 26, the *Osservatore Romano* published the names of 70 consultants from all over the world.[7]

What follows is a review of publications related to the revision of the Church's law, insofar as they are concerned with general problems, particularly with the shape this codification should take and with the relation between canon law and the rest of the ecclesiastical sciences.

---

tinue the Council and the revision of the Codex: *AAS* 55 (1963), p. 572; cf. the encyclical *Ecclesiam Suam* of August 6, 1964, in *AAS* 56 (1964), p. 628; and Paulist Press Pamphlet (Glen Rock, N. J., 1964) Art. 46: "Naturally, it will be for the Council to suggest what reforms are to be introduced in the legislation of the Church. The post-concilliar commissions, especially the one instituted for the revision of canon law and already nominated by us, will formulate in concrete terms the deliberations of the ecumenical synod."

[5] *AAS* 55 (1963), pp. 363f.; *L'Osservatore Romano* of March 30 and April 6, 1963; *Documentation Catholique* 60 (1963), pp. 556–60; *La Croix* of March 30, 1963; the composition is as follows: from the Curia Cardinals Ciriaci (President, also President of the Commission for the Interpretation of the Codex and member of the Commission for the Codification of Oriental Law), Tisserant, Pizzardo, Masella, Cicognani, Copello, Agagianian, Valeri, Giobbe, Cento, Confalonieri, Marella, Testa, Antoniutti, Ottaviani, Roberti, Jullien, Larraona, Heard, Bea and Browne; from outside the curia, Cardinals Liénart, Ruffini, Quiroga Y Palacios, Léger, Montini, Urbani, Döpfner, Suenens, and shortly afterwards, Spellman; the Secretary was Giacomo Violardo, also Secretary to the Commission for the Interpretation of the Codex, now succeeded by R. Bidagor, S.J.

[6] Cardinals Alfrink, Meyer, Tappouni, Gilroy, De Barros Camara, Frings, Caggiano, Wyzsynski, Gracias, Koenig, Lefèbvre.

[7] 22 Bishops and 48 canonists—31 seculars, 16 regulars, and Prof. Pio Ciprotti.

II

AN ALPHABETICAL LIST OF PUBLICATIONS*

Abbo, J. "The Revision of the Code," in *The Jurist* 20 (1960), pp. 371–97.

Alvarez-Menendez, S. "Reseña juridico-canónica," in *Revista Española de Derecho Canónico* 14 (1959), pp. 123–30.

(Anonymous) "La Pontificia Commissione per la revisione del Codice di diritto canonico," in *L'Osservatore Romano* (April 6, 1963), p. 1ff.; French trs. in *La Documentation Catholique* 60 (1963), pp. 557–60.

Arza, A. "Tendencias de la legislación postcodicial," in *Estudios de Deusto* 9 (1961), pp. 151–79. This number contains the papers read at the VIII Semana de Derecho Canónico, held in the University of Deusto, September 1960, on the subject "La teoría general de la adaptación del Codigo de Derecho Canónico."

Barion, H. "Die gegenwärtige Lage der Wissenschaft von katholischen Kirchenrecht," in *Zeitschrift für evangelisches Kirchenrecht* 8 (1962), pp. 228–90.

Bernhard, J. "En vue de la réforme du droit canonique," in *Revue de droit canonique* 13 (1963), pp. 135–48.

Bibliophilus, "Post annos decem a Codicis applicatione," in *Jus Pontificium* 8 (1928), pp. 137–42.

Bonet, E. "Perspectiva de la adaptación de la disciplina del Codigo Derecho Canónico," in *Estudios de Deusto* 9 (1961), pp. 9–17.

Breydy, M. "Diálogo canónico entre orientales y occidentales," in *Estudios de Deusto* 9 (1961), pp. 140–50.

Cabreros de Anta, M. "La revisión del Codigo de Derecho Canónico," in *Illustración del Clero* 53 (1960), pp. 384–94; "Algunas reformas de la legislación eclesiastica," in *Rev. Españ. de Derecho Canónico* 19 (1964), pp. 177–90.

Cann, H. "Changing Emphases in the Concept of Authority in the Church," in *The Jurist* 23 (1963), pp. 377–93.

Ciprotti, P. *Osservazioni al testo del Codex Juris Canonici* (Città del Vaticano, 1944); *Observaciónes al texto del Codex Juris Canonici.* (Salamanca, 1950); "De vocabulorum usu ad ius subiectivum designandum in Codice Iuris Canonici," in *Acta congressus internationalis juris canonici, Romae, 25–30 Septembris, 1950.* Rome, 1953 pp. 57–61 and in *Ephemerides Juris Canonici* 8 (1952), pp. 129–33; "De arte leges ferendi in Ecclesia; Investigación y elaboración del Derecho Canónico," in *Trabajos de la V semana de Derecho Canónico* (Barcelona, etc., 1956), pp. 333–6; "Il Codice di Diritto Canonico e il suo aggiornamento," *Eph. Juris Can.* 17 (1961), pp. 9–21.

Dammert Bellido, J. "¿Es aplicable la legislación canónica en America Latina?" in *Rev. Esp. de Derecho Canónico* 17 (1962), pp. 513–23.

* References to these works will appear in abbreviated form in the rest of the article.

De Brie, G. "De bijbelse radicalisering van de wet," in *Tijdschrift voor theologie* 3 (1963), pp. 139–65.

De Echeverria, L. "El lenguaje en el Codex Juris Canonici," in *Eph. Juris Can.* 3 (1947), pp. 429–56; "Aspectos sociológicos de la adaptación del Código," in *Estudios de Deusto* 9 (1961), pp. 258–73.

Di Jorio, A. "L'aggiornamento del Codice di diritto canonico," in *Laurentianum* 3 (1962), pp. 417–42.

Dumon, W. "Bij de Codex-herziening," in *Collationes Brugenses et Gandavenses* 10 (1964), pp. 49–67.

Espin Canovas, D. "Lecciones de las codifiaciones civiles," in *Estudios de Deusto* 9 (1961), pp. 86–96.

Eykemans, E. *De eigenaard van het kanoniek recht en de herziening van de Codex Juris Canonici.* Nijmegen, 1961.

Goyeneche, S. "Balance de la codificación," in *Estudios de Deusto* 9 (1961), pp. 97–118.

Huizing, P. "Plannen van paus Joannes XXIII met het kerkelijk recht," in *De Maasbode* (February 13, 1959) and in *Katholiek Archief* 14 (1959), pp. 252–6; "Over kanoniek godsdienstige wetten," in *Nederlandse Katholieke Stemmen* 53 (1962), pp. 323–8.

Jiménez-Urresti, T. "La problemática de la adaptación del Derecho Canónico en perspectiva ecumenista," in *Estudios de Deusto* 9 (1961), pp. 274–362.

Jombart, E. "Tradition et progrès en droit canonique," in *Actes du congrès de droit canonique* (Paris, 1950), pp. 295–304.

Keller, H. "Wandlungen und Mängel kirchlicher Gesetze. Papstäusserungen und Thomastexte," in *Miscellanea iuridica Iustiniani et Gregorii IX legibus commemorandis.* Analecta Gregoriana VIII (Rome, 1935), pp. 7–50.

Kemmeren, G. "Hedendaagse stromingen in de kerkelijke rechtswetenschap," in *Tijdschrift voor theologie* 3 (1963), pp. 361–77; "Crisis ten aanzien van het kerkelijk recht," in *De Nieuwe Mens* 15 (1963/1964), pp. 217–25.

Klok, J. "De herziening van de Codex Juris Canonici," in *Diocesaan tijdschrift voor het bisdom Luik* 49 (1963), pp. 30–41.

Lio, E. "Metodologia giuridica e costituzioni del Sinodo di Roma," in *L'Osservatore Romano* (January 31, 1960).

Lombardia, P. "La sistemática del Codex y su posible adaptación." in *Estudios de Deusto* 9 (1961), pp. 213–37.

Losada Cosmes, R. "Reformas legislativas en la historia de la Iglesia," in *Estudios de Deusto* 9 (1961), pp. 18–85.

McManus, F. "The Second Vatican Council and the Canon Law," in *The Jurist* 22 (1962), pp. 259–86.

Mörsdorf, K. "Die Stellung der Laien in der Kirche," in *Revue de droit canonique* 10/11 (1960/61), pp. 214–34.

Örsy, L. "Vie de l'Eglise et renouveau du droit canonique," in *Nouvelle Revue Théologique* 85 (1963), pp. 952–65; "The Reform of Canon Law," in *The Clergy Review* 48 (1963), pp. 750–67; "Reform of Canon Law," in *America* 109 (Nov. 2, 1963), pp. 516f.; "Towards a Theological Conception of Canon Law," in *The Jurist* 24 (1964), pp. 383–92.

Perez Mier, L. "La adaptación del derecho económico," in *Estudios de Deusto* 9 (1961), pp. 238–58.

Primetshofer, B. "Der Weg der Kirche ins 21. Jahrhundert und das kanonische Recht," in *Der Seelsorger* 33 (1963), pp. 515–22.

Pujol Villegas, C. "Lecciones de la codificación canónica oriental (en vistas de una revisión del Código de Derecho latino)," in *Estudios de Deusto* 9 (1961), pp. 119–39.

Schmitz, H. *Die Gesetzessystematik des Codex Juris Canonici Liber I–III.* Münchener Theologische Studien, Kanonistische Abteilung 18 (Munich, 1963).

Spectator, "Post annos 15 a Codicis J. C. promulgatione," in *Jus Pontificium* 12 (1932), pp. 177–85.

(Francis Cardinal Spellman), *Proposita de codice juris canonici revisendo* (with a *praefatio* by Francis Cardinal Spellman) (New York, May 1963).

Stokes, E. "The 'Aggiornamento' of the Code of Canon Law," in *Chicago Studies* 2 (1963), pp. 283ff.

Szentirmai, A. "Die Bedeutung des römischen Diözesansynode für die Kanonistik," in *Theol. u. Glaube* 51 (1961), pp. 215–33; "Zur bevorstehenden Reform des Kanonischen Rechts. Vorschläge und Entwicklungstendenzen," in *Archiv des öffentlichen Rechts* 87 (1962), pp. 67–81; "The Legal Language of the New Code of Canon Law of the Oriental Churches," in *The Jurist* 22 (1962), pp. 39–70.

Tibau, N. "El Código de Derecho Canónico postconciliar," in *Christus* (Mexico, 1964), pp. 397–402.

Useros Carretero, M. "De jure canonico in vita Ecclesiae eiusque adaptatione sub lumine Legis Novae annotationes," in *Rev. Esp. de Derecho Canónico* 18 (1963), pp. 658–65.

Van Bilsen, B. "Pastorale herbouw van het kerkelijk recht," in *De Nieuwe Mens* 15 (1963/4), pp. 226–30.

Van Hove, A. *Prolegomena* (2nd ed. Malines-Rome, 1945).

Wahner, G. "El lenguaje del Código," in *Estudios de Deusto* 9 (1961), pp. 180–212.

Winninger, P. "L'adaptation du Code aux exigences pastorales," in *Estudios de Deusto* 9 (1961), pp. 385–98.

III

UPDATING THE CODEX JURIS CANONICI

To bring the Codex up to date, we should begin by applying the regulation laid down by Benedict XV that all new general laws and all modifications of existing general law should be regularly inserted in the Code.[8] So far this has never been done, al-

[8] *Motu Proprio: Cum Codicis Juris Canonici,* in *Codex Juris Canonici,* p. LI.

though particularly since Pius XII, numerous additions and modifications have appeared, such as those concerned with the papal election, the enclosure of convents for female religious, the secular institutes, the extraordinary minister of confirmation, the eucharistic fast, fasting and abstinence, the canonical form of marriage for children of non-Catholics, baptized as Catholics but not educated as such, the permission required for the alienation of ecclesiastical property and the various additions to and modifications of the ecclesiastical penal code.[9]

Apart from this, very many canons have been more closely defined, interpreted or extended in the instructions, decrees and replies given by various Roman Congregations and the Commission for the Interpretation of Canon Law and the jurisprudence of the Rota. A better formulation of these points may result.[10]

Although there is no official up-to-date edition of the Code, editions have appeared periodically in which the authors indicated for each cannon the relevant documents appearing after the promulgation of the Code.[11] The general revision of canon law necessarily implies that both the canons and the new documents be incorporated.

IV

TECHNICAL IMPROVEMENT

The matter of *technical improvement* of the Codex was raised soon after its publication.[12] Instead of using the same name for

---

[9] Ciprotti, *Il Codice*, pp. 12f.; Abbo, pp. 383-90; Dumon, pp. 53-8; Metz, pp. 52f.; Klok, pp. 33-5.

[10] Ciprotti, *Il Codice*, p. 11; Abbo, pp. 378-83.

[11] E. Regatillo, *Interpretatio et jurisprudentia Codicis juris canonici;* C. Sartori, *Enchiridion canonicum seu S. Sedis responsiones post editum Codicem J. C. datae;* T. Bouscaren, *The Canon Law Digest. Officially Published Documents Affecting the Code of Canon Law;* S. Meyer, *Neueste Kirchenrechtssammlung.*

[12] The best known critics were U. Stutz, *Der Geist des Codex juris canonici* (Stuttgart, 1918) and M. Falco, *Introduzione allo studio del Codex Juris Canonici* (Turin, 1925); cf. Bibliophilus; Keller; Jombart; Van Hove, p. 625, n. 566; K. Mörsdorf, "Codex Juris Canonici," in *Staatslexikon,* II, 2nd ed. p. 1247.

the same juridical concepts and of indicating different notions by different terminology, the Codex hardly ever reserves one term for one concept and often uses different terms for the same concept.[13] The consultants of the preparatory commission were instructed to preserve the terminology of the sources as faithfully as possible, in spite of temporal and local difference; the idea was to preserve the traditional interpretation together with the terminology.[14] The style, too, of the various parts is not homogeneous because the final draft of the projects was undertaken by different editors.[15]

Aids for this kind of work are provided by the canonical dictionary composed by Rudolf Köstler[16] and especially by the index of all the terms used in the Codex, drawn up by A. Lauer.[17] The first to deal with this problem systematically was Mörsdorf whose dissertation has been referred to above (see footnote 13). The Secretary of the Commission for the Codification of Oriental Law, A. Cardinal Coussa, persuaded his collaborator, Prof. Pio Ciprotti, to publish his valuable observations on every aspect of this technical improvement.[18] De Echeverrìa remarked [19] that, among other things, he liked to see not neo-Latin, but rather

[13] K. Mörsdorf, *Die Rechtssprache des Codex Juris Canonici* (Paderborn, 1937) p. 23.

[14] Van Hove, p. 625, n. 566, note 2; F. Roberti, "Il Cardinal Pietro Gasparri. L'uomo, il sacerdote, il diplomatico, il giurista," in *Apollinaris* 33 (1960), p. 42; Goyeneche, p. 117, n. 28.

[15] Van Hove, *ibid.;* the demand for a *Codex repetitae praelectionis,* on the pattern of Justinian's Code, is typical.

[16] *Wörterbuch zum C.I.C.* (Munich, 1929-1930).

[17] (Francis Cardinal Spellman), on p. IV, suggests that a commission be set up of canonists, theologians and Latinists to see to it that the preliminary work on the new Codex uses a consistent and accurate terminology. The cardinal wants them to use a computer which would indicate in the shortest time how often and where each word is used, and observes that an American university already uses computers for this kind of work. Too great uniformity of words and ambiguity in the use of words could be avoided if the Latin Codex followed the Oriental Codex in introducing a *titulus* "De verborum significatione". Schmitz, however, is against such a separate section.

[18] *Osservazioni;* the second, Spanish edition and Ciprotti's other studies all deal with this subject.

[19] *El Lenguaje,* pp. 433-5; Goyeneche, p. 116; Wahner, p. 182.

the replacement of traditional canonical terms by classical Roman terminology. Gotthard Wahner observes that it should be made clearer what is ordered and what is advised; what is impermissible and what is also invalid.[20]

In this work it is particularly important to realize that *canonical* concepts, which envisage actions, are not the same as *philosophical* or *theological* concepts, which signify realities.[21] To give one simple example: since very many norms concerning bishops also apply to abbots and prelates *nullius*, these latter groups are simply covered in canon law by the concept "bishop".[22] There is obviously no point in discussing whether this canonical concept is "accurate" but rather whether it is, in fact, "practical", *i.e.*, whether it clarifies the norms. Here lies the whole "secret" of that notorious "legal fiction", often so curiously misunderstood by canonists whose scholastic formation surpasses their juridical training.[23]

[20] *Ibid.*, p. 203; cf. Abbo, pp. 375–8.

[21] T. Jiménez-Urresti, "Ciencia y teología del derecho canónico, o la lógica jurídica y lógica teológica," in *Lumen*, (Vitoria, 1959), pp. 140–55; P. Huizing, "De 'positivismo' quodam iuridico nota practica," in *Periodica* 48 (1959), pp. 77–100; "A Practical Note on a Type of Juridical 'Positivism'," in *The Catholic Lawyer* 7 (1961-2), pp. 11–23.

[22] Canon 215, §2; A. Felici, "De extensione nominis episcopi abbatibus et praelatibus (!) nullius," in *Apollinaris* 36 (1963), pp. 298–320, shows how the consistent application of such a simple fiction simplifies matters considerably.

[23] The loose handling of practical juridical notions as of "real" (metaphysical!) notions is a constant source of confusion in canon law. Thus, for instance in the discussion of the terms "public" and "private" (soundly criticized by Wahner, in his section on "sociological and linguistic adjustment", pp. 207-12); or in the case of the "legal person" (cf. *Periodica* 48, 1959, pp. 213-28, where the "reality" of a given pursuit is confused with the juridical fiction of "personality" attributed to it, and where this fiction is gratuitously supposed to have "disastrous consequences"); or again in the use of the idea of "ius" (as in *Periodica* 49, 1960, p. 454, footnote 17: every system of positive law must take over the metaphysical notion of "ius" under pain of falling into positivism and nominalism!); or again the notion of "ius" in itself (the "substance" of a right) which remains even when the exercise of the right is temporarily suspended; this is used by jurists to indicate that after the interruption the right does not have to be granted afresh, but that this right is revived on a basis similar to what it first had; but this is constantly confused with a "metaphysical" substance, etc.

V

DEVELOPMENT OF THE CODE

The *system* of the Code, fifty years ago, was still bound to be based on what was taken over in canon law from Gaius's Institutiones (*personae, res, actiones:* persons, things and actions) via Justinian (*personae, res, iudices, crimina:* persons, things, judges and crimes) together with Lancelotti's *Institutiones juris canonici,* since 1563. The key notion was that *jus* equalled "legal rights". The Codex is composed of five "books"; I General Norms; II Persons; III Things; IV Procedure; V Legal Offenses and Penalties. Of these, books II to V would correspond to: II Those subject to the law (modelled on Napoleon's *Code civil* and its successors); III Objects with which the law deals; IV The elements contained in legal procedure, and V How to deal with violations of the law.[24]

Wahner considers this system both adequate and elegant, though he admits that another division, from the ecclesiastical point of view for instance, might be preferable as long as it is just as perfect.[25]

Lombardía wants a harmonious relationship between the contents or spirit of a given juridical order and the structure of the Code which expresses it. This relationship need not be scientific but must be practical, clear and able to convey the spirit of the ecclesiastical community. He does not seek to link it up with the technique of civil codes, which has given rise to many difficulties in the Code, but rather with the canonical tradition. Like the medieval decretals the Code should open with a *titulus* (group of chapters) on *God as law-giver and divine law* so as to indicate how one should appeal to it in practice, and also in order to give the study of canon law a less technical and a more philosophical and theological slant. Some of the norms now found in Book II,

[24] Van Hove, p. 623ff., n. 565; Lombardía, pp. 222–9; Wahner, p. 201, n. 54.

[25] *Ibid.,* p. 201, n. 54 and footnote 94.

such as those concerning physical and legal persons, procedure, the rights of the clergy, *and* those of the laity—with whom, at present, not a single canon deals exclusively!—should be put in Book I, *General Norms.* The section about the clergy in general and in particular *(De clericis in genere* and *in specie)* is not a matter of personal law but of constitutional law and deals with the ecclesiastical hierarchy in general and in particular. The sections on religious and lay people (*De religiosis* and *De laicis*) might well be moved to Book III, *Ecclesiastical Organizations,* religious and others. The *res* ("things") of the present 3rd Book are, according to the 1st canon, 726, not legal objects but "means by which the Church achieves her purpose". It has long been pointed out that this peculiar notion serves as an umbrella under which all manner of wholly heterogeneous elements find shelter.[26] Lombardía suggests that this section should be divided into five separate books: IV, the *Sacraments;* V, *Sacred Places, Objects and Seasons;* VI, *Worship;* VII, *Ecclesiastical Doctrinal Authority,* and VIII, *Ecclesiastical Property.* Lastly, Book IX on *Legal Offenses and Penalties* ought to precede X on *Legal Procedure.*

Schmitz, too, wants to put the general norms of personal law and the statutes of limitation (*verjaring*) in Book I. Book II, *The Structure of the Church (Verfassungsrecht)* should contain a general section on the clergy (including the laws about benefices) and the laity, and a particular section dealing with (1) the government of the universal Church; (2) the particular Churches; (3) the religious; (4) the organizations. He is particularly opposed to the present threefold division into clergy, religious and laity.[27] The heterogeneous items of Book III should not be lumped together as "things", but be brought together under a section on administrative law under the three headings of: 1. worship (including the sacraments), 2. ecclesiastical doctrinal authority and 3. Church property.[28]

[26] Wahner's suggestion on p. 201, n. 54, "Res sunt media *in hoc libro* recensita," is a logical improvement but not practical.

[27] So does Mörsdorf; see his article "Laie," in *Lexikon für Theologie und Kirche,* Vol. 6 (2nd ed.), p. 741.

[28] Schmitz, pp. 347–55, gives a complete new plan for the division of Books I–III; Wahner, pp. 202f., deals with the plan of Bk. IV.

Useros, professor at the Institute for Pastoral Theology at the University of Salamanca, starts from the three aspects of ecclesial activity as initiated by Christ: the preaching of the Gospel, the building up of the Church by means of the sacraments and the Church's official pastoral mission. Each of these three functions is then further determined by the Church's authorities on the following lines: (1) the Word of God, its preservation and proclamation by the Church; (2) the sacraments and their administration; (3) the servants of the Church in their pastoral function on three levels: (a) that of the universal Church; (b) that of the diocese, and (c) that of the parish; (4) the various positions in the Church: (a) the religious, and (b) the laity; (5) the rules for procedure; (6) the maintenance of discipline or ecclesiastical sanctions; (7) the glorification of the faithful death by the Church. This plan shows at once the connection of the Church's nature with the regulation of her activities, which is important from both pastoral and ecumenical points of view. The various chapters should indicate clearly which regulations are of divine and which of human origin.[29]

It is indeed desirable to refrain from erecting a system of canon law upon concepts derived from civil law or from constitutional and administrative law in the State. In recent years many theologians and canonists have studied the specific character of canon law.[30] At first they started with the thesis that law has to do with regulating the outward life of the community, the State doing this in the natural sphere, the Church in the supernatural sphere. Today the difference between the two is seen as something more concrete and fundamental. The ecclesial community is founded

[29] *De iure, passim.*

[30] Literature and survey of the various tendencies in M. Useros Carretero, *"Statuta Ecclesiae" y "Sacramenta Ecclesiae" en la eclesiologia de St. Tomas de Aquino. Reflexion tomista sobre el Derecho de la Iglesia en paralelismo a la actual tematica eclesiologico-canonica* (Rome, 1962); "Temática relevante en los estudios actuales sobre la naturaleza peculiar del ordenamiento canónico," in *Revista Española de Derecho Canónico* 14 (1959), pp. 73–120; C. Kemmeren, *Hedendaagse stromingen en Ecclesia et Jus. Analysis critica operum Josephi Klein* (Rome, 1962); P. Fedele, "La teoria generale del diritto canonico. Letteratura dell' ultimo decennio," in *Ephemerides Juris Canonici* 19 (1963), pp. 9–86.

on Christ's triple mandate: sacramental sanctification, preaching and pastoral office, the last being wholly determined by the first two. The concrete and exclusive nature of canon law is that it regulates the administration of Christ's saving mysteries and the preaching of his word in his name and in virtue of his mandate. It is not just the salvation of souls (*salus animarum*) without further qualification, but rather the salvation of souls in the apostolic tradition of Christ's dispensation of salvation.

It is these ideas which determine the contents, the extent and the limitations of canon law, and specifically of Catholic canon law. On the basis of these ideas a truly organic system of canon law can be worked out.

VI
LEGAL CODE OR CONSTITUTION

Ciprotti thinks that the most typical feature of the Codex— already beginning with Trent, but constant since the 19th century —is the tendency toward a gradual, though moderate, centralization of power, *i.e.*, the decrease in power formerly possessed by lesser institutions, particularly by the metropolitans and the provincial councils, and the reinforcement of heirarchical subordination. He also points out that the elasticity and flexibility of Church laws allowed them to remain operative for a very long period among nations with broad geographical and ethnical differences.[31] Goyeneche considers that one of the most valuable results of the Codex is the *unidad efectiva su disciplina* (the effective unity of its discipline); it is the one law which governs the Latin Church from one end of the world to the other. Both rulers and ruled find definite norms for their actions in the Codex, whether in Europe, America, Asia, Africa or Oceania.

The Codex itself contributed to this maintenance of unity by its determined opposition to particular laws and customs, even from time immemorial, by abolishing the communication of

[31] *Il Codice*, pp. 9f.

privileges or the revocation of a large number of them and by prohibiting ordinaries from granting dispensations in general law. This tendency was reinforced by the commission for the interpretation of the Codex. According to Goyeneche this unity of discipline powerfully contributed to the creation of one bond of love: one powerful juridical structure gave the people an almost ineradicable feeling of belonging together, as Roman law showed in history. This unity, brought about by the codification of Latin law, has had a decisive influence on the codification of Oriental law.[32]

The factual complaints of José Dammert Bellido, Bishop of Cajamarca, Peru, cast more effective doubt on this unqualified praise of unity than mere theories. After explaining the difficulties created by canonical norms in matters of parishes, obligation of residence, catechetics, marriage, the Sunday and Easter duties, the breviary, the prohibition of medical practice by the clergy, the quinquennial report, episcopal ceremonial, diocesan curia, liturgy, church music, seminaries and the Latin language, he concludes that for a canonist who also has the pastoral care of 419,000 souls spread over 15,000 square kilometers with 37 priests of whom 15 are left to cope with 337,000 rural Christians, the situation is oppressive and, humanly speaking, hopeless. He wrote in the hope that theologians and canonists would draft a project of legislation suitable for such a situation, stripped of accidental superfluities and true to the great principles of the Church.

These theologians and canonists are already at work on this, either within the framework of one Code, or in a more pluralistic arrangement.

Abbo considers that a revised Codex could well devote a large section to missionary law and to exceptional circumstances such as might exist in parts of the Church subject to a hostile government and where the hierarchy cannot communicate with Rome. Insofar as missionary law is concerned, a codification of the numerous norms of a general bearing, provided by the Propa-

[32] *Ibid.*, pp. 105–7, nn. 12–14; cf. Van Hove, pp. 622f., n. 564.

ganda before and after the publication of the Codex, would be invaluable. Many are opposed to this, but others emphatically support the possibility and necessity of a general law, both liturgical and disciplinary, which would meet the requirements of life in the missions. Such a codification should not prove difficult.[33]

Pojol takes the codification of Oriental law as an example. It tends toward unity of law, but as far as possible respects the law and customs of each Church and maintains a certain diversity within unity. Latin law would have to become more supple, a development which would demand more respect for the different customs and ways of life of so many different nations. Otherwise it would smother all that is good in their traditions and sterilize much of their native vitality.[34] Cabreros takes the line that the revision will be universalist, concentrating rather on the Church as a whole, because the Codex should be valid for the whole Church. But the various needs of the Church are better known now than fifty years ago. Hence some of the laws will have to become more elastic, or exceptions must be foreseen in the law itself, or the execution will have to be made dependent on local authorities or on interdiocesan consultation.[35] Arza noted a tendency toward "limited universality" already in the legislation after the promulgation of the Codex. For instance, in the laws concerning fasting and abstinence and evening masses, the application or obligation of the general law was left to the decision of the bishops.[36]

Winninger thinks that one single Codex which would apply to so many different people is no longer possible. "Catholicity" is no longer an empty notion, but a concrete experience. The

---

[33] *Ibid.*, pp. 391f., with reference to Paventi, *Breviarium iuris missionum* (Rome, 1952); De Reeper, *A Missionary Companion* (Westminster, Md., 1952); Bartocetti, *Jus constitutionale missionum* (Turin, 1947); L. Buys, "De adaptatione juris canonici praesertim in missionibus," in *Studia missionalia* VII (Rome, 1953), pp. 241–68 (on the possbilities of adaptation within the existing law), and above all, Hernandez, *Adaptación misionera* (Bilbao, 1958), pp. 425-50.

[34] *Ibid.*, p. 125.

[35] La adaptación del libro primero del Código de Derecho Canónico," in *Estudios de Deusto* 9 (1961), p. 367.

[36] *Ibid.*, pp. 160f.

various circumstances, mentality and degree of development of the various Churches demand different regimes. The Codex should be a "constitution", containing only norms that are fundamental and universally applicable, and no others (particularly no pastoral norms) such as those concerned with parochial organization or the status of the clergy. Between the general constitution for the whole Church and the diocesan statutes he wants to introduce regional codices, for specific countries or groups of countries. These should take account of existing concordats and of such civil laws as are pastorally important (for instance: concerning schools, the relation between parish and municipality and the status of the clergy).

On the point of personal rights some legislative systems are ahead of canon law, and canon law could let itself be influenced by these as it was formerly influenced by Roman and other law.[37] According to Useros, divine law does not demand uniformity. Pastoral concern is more important than legal unity. It would be desirable that, like the missions and the Oriental Churches, other regions and provinces of the Church should also have their own particular laws.[38] On the basis of a correct theology of law, De Brie thinks it important that justice should be done to the principle of pluriformity, not only in the new Churches, but also in the old ones. Experience has shown, particularly in mission countries, that general legislation brings grave difficulties with it if it does not limit itself to essentials that are indeed universally applicable. If it goes into too great detail, it must take account of many special circumstances which disqualify it *ipso facto* as a world-law. Exceptions may be necessary in law, but are better left to local authorities such as bishops or episcopal conferences. How much decentralization there should be is a matter of juridical organization and technique.[39]

Others, starting from general law, have reached similar conclusions. Örsy points out that in civil law not every law carries

[37] *Ibid.,* pp. 386f.
[38] *Ibid.,* p. 664.
[39] *Ibid.,* pp. 144f.

the same weight. Most authoritative is the constitution, which can be modified only with great difficulty. Then come the laws usually passed by Parliament. Lastly, there are the regulations which are made or modified by lower authorities. The one Codex of Canon Law is supposed to contain all the general laws, from important and fundamental ones (such as the convocation of a general council) to rather unimportant ones (such as those concerning the ceremonial for a funeral). Both kinds enjoy the same authority, the same force and the same technical stability.

Whoever touches one single point of the law about legal procedure, touches the Codex as a whole. In countries which follow the "Common Law" of England, the higher tribunals themselves lay down the procedure; "Common Law" lays down only the principles by which justice must be administered.[40] The right kind of codification should include all the fixed legal norms concerning the codified matter, so that no special laws are required on these points, but it should exclude subsidiary or executive norms whose regulation should not be prescribed by law.[41] Ciprotti, too, maintains that regulations which are too variable, such as those that depend on the changing value of currency, and too detailed, such as those contained in canons 378 and 379, §§ 3 and 4, concerning archives, do not belong in the law but should be contained in separate instructions or rules. This is particularly true for the Church where there are great local differences and where the local authority must be respected.[42]

In this connection we should take note of De Brie's observation that the repeated changes, within less than fifteen years, about fasting and abstinence, the eucharistic fast, evening Masses, the celebration of Easter, etc., have raised doubts about how seriously the Church's law has to be taken. If positive legislation

---

[40] *Reform*, pp. 515f.; *Vie*, pp. 953, 959, 964f.; Kemmeren, *Crisis*, p. 220; Espin, p. 93; McManus, p. 284.

[41] Espin, pp. 91f.

[42] *De arte*, p. 335, which deals with the well-known dilemma between legal *certainty*, which is greater as *more* is laid down in the general law, and the certainty of *law*, which increases as more is left to ordinaries and judges in concrete cases; there is no "perfect solution" for this.

must be taken seriously and be effective, it must be backed by a sound tradition. "Quid leges sine moribus?" (What is the use of laws if there are no customs?)[43] Arza points out that the tendency of the new legislation to make the introduction of it dependent on the bishops, aims precisely at a gradual transition.[44]

From the ecumenical point of view Breydy has pointed out that there is no single constitution for the whole Church: there are two papal legislative systems for specific Churches, the Latin and the Oriental. There could be more. Thus, a Protestant community that would like to unite with the Catholic could be given a special papal statute.[45] It is even possible to have one constitution for the whole Church which would contain only the fundamental norms of her constitution, and would be supplemented with special general statutes for the Latin Church, the Oriental Church, the new Churches, the Churches that are cut off from Rome and possibly others still.

VII
A CODEX OR A CHURCH ORDER?

When one compares the ancient canonical collections, from Dionysius Exiguus to Gratian, with the canons of the present Code, it is obvious that these two collections are totally different in character. The ancients collected complete texts of popes, councils, Fathers of the Church, etc., which often related the facts leading up to the document in question and gave the reasons for the rules, decisions or advice given. In the early Church and in the early Middle Ages these ecclesiastical regulations were contrasted as "sacred canons" to the "laws" of emperors and kings. The notion of canon law and Church laws dates only from the time when a more centralized Church saw herself as an organized society in contrast to the States.

The consultants of the commission, charged with the prepara-

---

43 *Ibid.*, pp. 140f.
44 *Ibid.*, p. 160.
45 *Ibid.*, p. 141.

tion of the Codex, were instructed to extract only disciplinary regulations from the sources (without excluding a few principles of natural law and of faith), and to take from these regulations only the legally relevant part, the actual regulation, without the factual introduction or the motives, and to word this in concise formulae. In this they followed the codification of civil law.[46] That is why the vast majority of dogmatic items, which occupied such a large place in the older collections, has fallen out. There are, nevertheless, those who object that the Code still contains norms concerning dogma and morality. Roberti counters this objection by pointing out that though law is distinct from dogma and morality, it is wrong, even from the scientific point of view, to follow the popular fashion of separating law from faith and morals, because it deprives law of its natural roots.[47]

Some also criticize the exhortatory form of several canons on the ground that this should not be done in a system of law which ought only to contain prohibitions, permissions, regulations and stipulations.[48] Others have replied that the exhortatory form is sometimes equivalent to a command, and even when this is not the case, there can still be legal consequence since in some cases the higher authority can allow a lower authority to command what has been advised from a higher hand.[49] Moreover, the legislator of the Codex is also head of the Church, with other and more important tasks than legislation; he may have wanted to express certain things on a basis other than that of his legal power *in foro externo.*[50]

In connection with the Roman Synod reference has been made

[46] Van Hove, *op. cit.*, pp. 622f., n. 564; pp. 623f., n. 565; Goyeneche, p. 100; Ciprotti, *Il Codice*, p. 10.

[47] Cf. *supra*, footnote 14; Goyeneche, p. 117, n. 28.

[48] Can. 134: the recommendation of communal life for the clergy; Can. 348, §2: the recommendation given to titular bishops to offer Mass for their diocese from time to time; Can. 744: about informing the bishop beforehand about the baptism of adults, and his administering this baptism if he so wishes; Can. 790: about administering confirmation during Pentecost week, etc.

[49] Van Hove, *op. cit.*, p. 625, n. 566.

[50] Ciprotti, *De arte*, p. 334; *Lezioni di diritto canonico* (Padua, 1944), pp. 40–2, nn. 34–5.

to the great canonist, Benedict XIV, who said that the statutes of
a diocesan synod must not only command, forbid and punish, but
also exhort, warn and instruct, and these elements acquire thereby
a kind of authority of their own.[51] Article 5, § 1 of this synod says:
"The wording of the various articles shows what kind of obligation is involved," and §2 adds: "Exhortations, too, must be
obediently accepted." From these two texts the conclusion has
been drawn that canon law contains both canonical commands
and canonical exhortations, that it knows both a "must" and
an "it behooves", the reason being that in these terms there is
no difference between an obligation in law and an obligation in
conscience. It is even said that present canon law considers the
obligation in conscience as the most important sanction. And
this would explain why the synod has said so little about penalties.[52]

There is obviously no point in approaching the complex set of
rules which we now call canon *law* from the angle of a philosophical or other *a priori* notion of law in order to eliminate whatever
would not correspond to such a notion. But there is a point in
asking whether the concrete Church order, such as it has developed historically, is the same type of order as that prevailing in
the secular State. This Church order contains many regulations
which determine legal situations both in the domain of the temporal, such as the right to a livelihood in the exercise of an ecclesiastical office, and in the domain of the spiritual, such as the
right to administer or receive the sacraments. Apart from these
regulations there are many others which do not determine legal
situations but impose personal religious obligations, such as fasting and abstinence, the reciting of the breviary, monastic rules,

---

[51] Lio.

[52] Szentirmai, *Bedeutung,* pp. 216 and 221f., with reference to same,
"Der Umfang der verpflichtenden Kraft des Gesetzes im kanonischen
Recht," in *Archiv des öffentlichen Rechts* 85 (1960), pp. 337ff.; G.
Michiels, *Normae generales juris canonici* I (2nd ed., 1949), pp. 290ff.;
P. G. Caron, "Il valore giuridico delle esortazioni del Legislatore nel
diritto canonico," in *Studi in onore di Vincenzo del Giudice,* I (Milan,
1952).

etc.[53] The legal and religious regulations can be enforced, at least in principle, by sanctions, such as the loss of certain rights in the community or expulsion. Finally, there are a few regulations which advise, praise or warn against certains forms of behavior.

There is an essential difference between this Church order and that of civil law. The latter is a code of definite social behavior, sanctioned by the authorities. The Church order is a complex of regulations for religious behavior concerning the conditions or the right disposition for participation in the sacramental salvation of the community. The sacraments, indeed, are not merely the principal means, but actually constitute the Church as a community.[54] Canon law is the more detailed determination of this specific kind of religious activity by the ecclesiastical authority. It contains also legal situations and is therefore also a legal order, but this is not typical as it is of civil law.[55] It does not envisage principally and essentially the definition and maintenance of rights, but the ensurance of an ordered and worthy enactment of

[53] Huizing, *Over kanoniek . . . ; Jiménez-Urresti*, p. 333: extravagant and objectionable expressions such as the "juridical command" to hear Mass, of annual confession and communion, or the "juridical" power in matters of doctrine or over inward actions.

[54] *The Decree on Ecumenism of Vatican Council II*, Art. 22: baptism creates a "sacramental bond of unity" among all those baptized, aims at the full confession of the faith, the full incorporation in the Christ-willed institution of salvation and the eucharistic *communio;* see the *Constitution on the Church*, Art 3: ". . . in the sacrament of the eucharistic bread, the unity of all believers who form one body in Christ is both expressed and brought about;" and Art. 7: "Really partaking of the body of the Lord in the breaking of the eucharistic bread, we are taken up into communion with him and with one another. . . . In this way all of us are made members of his body, . . . 'but severally members one of another.' "

[55] Jimenez Urresti, pp. 333-5, points out rightly that the notion of "ius" is used analogically for the ordering of outward social life in Church and State; the moral obligation of Church law is an element of this order; whoever acts against it, loses his right to participation in the eucharistic community, and this right is not revived without reconciliation through the Church's authority (an element which Barion seems to overlook); civil law also obliges in conscience, but this obligation is not an element of this civil order; legally speaking, only the material observance of the contents of the law is relevant, and the secret violation of the law which cannot be legally established does not affect the legal position of the offender in law or in morality.

the community's worship. Here law serves religion. The wider term of "Church order" would be more suitable than canon "law", for the tendency to give the new Codex an exclusively "juridical" aspect would not correspond to its real character.

VIII
ARTICLES OF LAW OR "SACRED CANONS"?

What has been said implies the question whether the form chosen for the "canons", which is that of articles used in civil codes, is the best one for its purpose. It is said that canons are characterized by the fact that they are limited to command, prohibition and stipulation, leaving aside the occasion, purpose and motives (the *ratio legis*, the reason for the law).[56] This applies to the canons of the Codex, but is not the original meaning. "Canon" means rule or norm. We speak of the rule of faith and morals (*regula fidei et morum*), contained in the "canon" of Holy Writ; we speak of the "canon" of the liturgy, as the rule for celebration. The Council of Nicaea (325) designates with the words "the ecclesiastical canon" all the regulations concerning the Church's life. This is perhaps the reason why the term "canon" was chosen and not "law", in order to distinguish the regulations of the Church, more persuasive than strictly compulsory, from the laws of the Empire.[57]

According to Ciprotti the modern form of the canon (*i.e.*, as an article of law) belongs to an art of legislation of which the ancient sources were ignorant.[58] But we may point out immediately that the abstract canon of today can be understood only if one knows its context in the older sources. For Ciprotti the most important rule of the art of legislation, or rather the rule which contains all other rules, is "clarity", and this not only for the jurists but, as far as possible, for all those who must obey or apply the law (which is not exactly made easier in canon law by the use

[56] Van Hove, pp. 623f., n. 565.
[57] Van Hove, pp. 40f., n. 40.
[58] *De arte*, p. 333.

of Latin).[59] Espin dislikes the technical language of the German codes, and prefers the French, which can be understood by all.[60]

But if the *ratio legis* (the reason for the law) in the Church order should belong to the norm itself, we may well wonder whether its omission does not impair the clarity which the norm requires. Kemmeren calls the formalism of the study of canon law one of the causes of the present crisis in canon law and of the general discomfort which it seems to rouse. The adage that the end of the law does not fall under the law (*finis legis non cadit sub lege*) is disastrous for canon law. In the teaching of it the law is explained apart from its meaning and purpose.[61] One might well apply here what Kemmeren says on the page before that referred to in the footnote: "We may even ask ourselves whether the law has not been formulated in a way which is too legalistic, too juridical and too little canonical." The formalism prevailing in the science of canon law corresponds to the formalistic way in which the Code is composed.

McManus's words are to the point here: the conciseness and precision of the canons are admirable qualities. They satisfy a need felt by both canonists and faithful. But it is precisely the usefulness of the Codex which makes us blind to the fact that now the sacred canons contain but bare regulations, give us, so to speak, only the end-product, while the motives, circumstances and intention of the law lie hidden in the original decretal or constitution. The question is serious, both for the study of the law and for the respect due to the legislator and his precepts. Motives and intention must be a support for the keeping of the law, but that can only be if they are expressed and known. To omit all this may be necessary for the conciseness of a Codex but must lead to a lack of appreciation for the reasonableness of the law.

Fortunately, this objection cannot be made to the new legislation. A good example is the constitution *Christus Dominus* of January 6, 1953, on the eucharistic fast and the evening Mass. It

[59] *Ibid.*
[60] *Ibid.*, p. 92.
[61] *Crisis*, pp. 220f.

sets out the history of, and the reasons for, the old law, and explains the circumstances and motives of the reform; not until the
end come the norms in the concise form of canons or of the regu-
lative section of a rescript. The decisions of the Council will no
doubt be drafted in the same way. Perhaps canonists could turn
their attention to this general problem, particularly in view of the
present state of the Codex and its reform. The reasons and fair-
ness of the law must be expressed in the way it is drafted.[62]

It is, indeed, more than desirable that the Church's legislation
be again based on the canon, in its classical meaning of "rule for
living", and not on the "article of law", the norm for the material
action. Not only what is materially determined, for instance, a
prescribed action, in a way that gives the essential, is concise and
at the same time clear, but the religious implication of such an
action must be treated in the same way, insofar as it is not obvious
from the prescribed action itself. Even in the secular society the
social context is of vital importance for the administration of law,
although it is there limited to the coercive ordering of outward
and materially legal actions. Within the Church the religious
meaning of the right to a bishop's See, to ecclesiastical property,
of the power to legislate, to bestow offices, etc., belongs to the
contents of that same right and power. Without this Christian religious content the whole edifice of canon law collapses like a
house of cards.[63]

The Roman synod tried to express its decisions not in a cold
fashion but with a certain "unction", indicating the motives and
using the language of persuasion, relying less on the power of the
legislator than on the meaningfulness and wisdom of his precepts.
To follow the "primitive" example of Gratian and his many predecessors and to introduce texts from the Gospel or the Fathers

[62] *Ibid.*, p. 272.

[63] An example of meaningful canonical treatment of religious norms is
given in B. Häring, "Das Breviergebet als Gesetz der Kirche im Geist-
gesetz des Lebens in Christus Jesus," in *Anima* 16 (1961), pp. 254–63;
for a summary of this, see *Nederlandse Katholieke Stemmen* 58 (1962),
pp. 115–9.

into canon law is no longer frowned upon precisely because this Church order is not a purely material and outward thing.[64]

IX

THE TASK OF THE CANONISTS

Recently a Dutch jurist expressed his amazement that the question was still asked whether criticism of current canon law is permissible. One would have to go back 150 years to find a jurist who would disapprove of criticism of civil law.[65] We do not have to go back that far in ecclesiastical circles. Authors like Falco, Stutz, Eichmann and Bernareggi have been upbraided for having criticized the Codex. Bibliophilus, who in 1928 began to publish in Rome an extremely cautious survey of criticisms of the Codex, thought it better (or was advised?) to stop this work and returned to it only five years later, as Spectator, and then still more cautiously. Even now an occasional canonist will speak only of an "accidental" adjustment of the Codex, such as the insertion of new legislation, the elimination of futile repetitions and the clarification of obscure texts; he would consider it arrogant to deal with substantial adjustment, the *ius condendum,* reserved to the legislator alone.[66] This attitude is now a thing of the past, but even a canonist of the caliber of Regatillo still thinks it necessary to cover his suggestions for a new Codex with the authority of Wernz and Capello, who also suggested some modifications, and to clothe them with assurances of submissive humility.[67] And he is not alone. On the other hand, it is obvious that any individual, however qualified, is aware that he can give only an opinion and will leave the enactment of a compulsory law to the respective authorities.

[64] Lio, *loc. cit.*
[65] *De positie van de verdachte in de kanonieke strafprocedure,* a report read by Prof. Mr. W. P. J. Pompe to the meeting of the juridical section of the *Thijmgenootschap* on March 3, 1962, p. 37.
[66] Alvarez, pp. 129f.
[67] *Ibid.,* pp. 299f.

For the rest, constructive criticism and suggestion are normal tasks of the science of canon law. The legislator cannot do without the information which free research alone can offer. From Dionysius to Peter Cardinal Gasparri he has been assisted in his legislative function by experts. Bonet considers it obvious that if the pope wants to introduce a reform, canonists must offer their services and do the preliminary scientific work.[68] Cassola reveals, with understandable satisfaction, that the offices of the Commission for the Interpretation of the Codex contain "a mass of observations and suggestions about the law which have come from everywhere and particularly from Masters in Canon Law (especially those of the Pontifical Institute of Canon Law, formerly at the palace of St Apollinaris, now in the Athenaeum of the Lateran)".[69]

In this connection McManus points out that, insofar as the reform of canon law is concerned, all Christian people have been asked repeatedly to express their *desiderata* during the preparations for the Council. This appeal to both clergy and laity is an appeal to public opinion, which Pius XII declared to be of vital importance for the Church.[70] Cabreros says that ecclesiastical authority, which alone is competent to execute this reform, announced it long before so that all could cooperate in the preparatory labors by modestly and respectfully offering various suggestions. When there is a need, the Church does not disdain public information but demands and seeks it.[71] Espin hints at the publication of the preliminary projects for a new Code so that use can be made of intelligent criticism.[72]

It is, however, precisely the behavior of the canonists which seems to cause a certain disquiet. Van Bilsen is wrong when he says that the revision commission is already functioning and doing so more or less alongside the Council as a kind of technical

[68] *Ibid.*, p. 11.
[69] O. Cassola, "De jure poenali Codicis canonico emendando," in *Apollinaris* 32 (1959), pp. 240-59, and 253.
[70] *Ibid.*, p. 259.
[71] *Estudios de Deusto* 9 (1961), p. 367.
[72] *Ibid.*, p. 93.

subsidiary business, which he thinks is most dangerous. One might nevertheless share his conviction that a purely technical and juridical incorporation of the new legislation and the conciliar decisions would not be very important, were it not that these decisions themselves are bound to lead to drastic changes. It is certainly true that others, besides canonists, should be interested in the place of canon law and in the overall structure of the Church's legislation.[73] One can go farther and say that practically every new canon will need the assistance of other experts.

The canonists, indeed, have only a relatively modest contribution to make. Ciprotti, a jurist and canonist with experience in this field, writes that, particularly in the technical process of drafting the law, all canonists must sharpen their wits in aid of the legislator.[74] The proper function of the canonist is, indeed, a technique rather than a science. The scientific study of the Church's reality in all its aspects is the function of the exegete, the patrologist, the historian, the theologian, the moralist, the liturgist, the sociologist, the missiologist, etc. The canonist is concerned only with the various ways in which this reality can be given a certain order by means of authoritative regulations. For instance, the theologian studies what the college of bishops *is,* and what must be the necessary relationship between pope and bishops as well as among themselves. The canonist examines the ways in which these relationships can be expressed coherently and conveniently in a set of ecclesiastical regulations. Pastoral theology establishes the best ways for the exercise of authority, for the administration of the sacraments and for the various forms of apostolate. The canonist investigates how far and which authoritative regulations are useful in bringing about the conclusions of pastoral theology in the community of the Church.[75] The canonist, therefore, constantly depends on others to find out what his set of regulations is supposed to achieve. By itself, the system is worthless.

[73] *Ibid.*, p. 227.
[74] *De arte*, p. 332.
[75] Cabreros, p. 368.

Hence the warnings against a canon law which is formalistic, self-sufficient, closed, and not based on dogma; against canonists who, while dealing with jurisdiction, forget that they are dealing with a communication of the power of the Spirit, in the biblical sense; who treat dioceses and parishes as administrative units from which the biblical image of shepherd and flock has vanished; who deal with the administration of Church property in a way which is divorced from its original purpose; against specialists, charged with the drafting, application and interpretation of Church laws, who are not sufficiently aware of Scripture, dogma and morality, and so run the risk of indulging in purely profane legalism.[76]

There seems to be a tendency in canon law to lock its whole value in its own structure; to chain a whole complex of laws to out-of-date legal concepts rather than link it up with the reality that it is supposed to regulate; to concentrate on the perfection of the system rather than on its adaptation to the character and needs of the community. This might bring with it the danger that coming revision will simply become a rewriting and re-regulating of old canons with an occasional nod toward modern developments in new fields, although the structure and form of the current system are meant for times gone by.

A completely new law is required, bearing on the contemporary condition of the Church's life and expressed in contemporary language; it should be closely linked with the new theology of the Church, inspired, not by collections of old canons, but by the present state of the ecclesiastical sciences which reflect the community whose life must be legislated for.[77] It has been pointed out that the new law must take note of the extraordinary development in pastoral insight which has been brought about by the providential movements of this century in catechetics, biblical science, liturgy, homiletics, and patristic studies; it must take into account

[76] Örsy, *Vie*, pp. 957f.
[77] Cann, pp. 392f.

the help provided by social sciences in the field of pastoral care; it must be aware of enormous problems such as the lack of priests in many places, and the consequences of this for such things as incardination and excardination.[78]

Bonet interprets Pope John's "aggiornamento" of the Codex, not as a revision but as an adaptation of the Church's discipline. This idea of "adaptation" is more closely related to social realities than to juridical techniques. In other words, this technique is something subordinate and functional, and must tend toward the communal welfare of the Church, the salvation of souls. And the primary communal fact to which the discipline of canon law should devote itself is the present Vatican Council.[79]

The rules which the canonists have to draft and the structures they have to project will be major contributions to the implementation of the Council's achievements. The vast treasure of knowledge and experience contained in the labor of thousands of bishops, religious superiors and their experts as well as in the work of the conciliar commissions have already provided the Commission for the Revision of the Code with a vast section of that varied reality for which they must frame regulations. Now, as in the years preceding the promulgation of the present Codex, the canonical experts surely will not be left to themselves and will not have to work amateurishly in all kinds of foreign territory. Opportunities will be found allowing them to be constantly in touch with bishops all over the world and with experts in all the other disciplines of the Church. The projects will be submitted to all the bishops, as happened in the case of the present Codex.[80] Theologians are expected to take part in the commissions.[81] The invitation could well be extended to experts in all other fields with which the Codex will be concerned.

[78] McManus, p. 277.
[79] Ibid., p. 9.
[80] (Spellman), p. IV.
[81] Örsy, Towards, p. 392.

X
A REAL CHURCH ORDER

The order which the new Codex must provide will have to be, above all, real. It must be realistic, workable and understandable for all concerned, and this is the task of the experts. It must be an order which governs the Church's life, which can be maintained and to which everyone can appeal, and this is the task of the canonists.

The first principle is that, before the technical and juridical norm is drafted, the social and human problem the norm is supposed to cover must be clearly and accurately set out.[82] What canonist has not had the painful experience of having to explain whole pieces of so-called canon law and to wade through entire treatises which lack any real value? Innumerable are the complaints about a law that cannot be "lived",[83] that is dead and cannot be applied;[84] about canonists who do not even ask themselves whether their "sentences" represent anything real.[85] The result is that some canonical practitioners, with more training in scholastic philosophy and theology than in their own subject, show little understanding of the necessary relation between their subject and real actions, even from the theoretical point of view.

Here, too, the rich times in which we live have brought about a welcome change. Arza has pointed to a definite social tendency in the most recent legislation: it does not merely deal, like the Codex, with "faithful", but with workers, soldiers, emigrants, students, mixed populations, political refugees, sailors, special groups such as the miners and steelworkers in Luxembourg and

[82] J. Ma. Setien, "Organización de las asociaciones sacerdotales," in *Revista Española de Derecho Canónico* 17 (1962), pp. 677–705: ". . . la persuasión de que antes de elaborar la fórmula jurídica, técnica, debe estar clara y bien definida la temática sociológica y humana a cuyo servicio debe ponerse la forma canónica que se quiera crear."

[83] McManus, p. 273.

[84] De Echeverría, *Aspectos*, pp. 264–6 and 267; Breydy, p. 149.

[85] Örsy, *Vie*, pp. 959f.

the dockworkers of Genoa. It takes account of the fact that more of life has shifted to night-time.[86] De Echeverría has drawn attention to the development of national and international institutions and the changes in diocesan ones.[87] Bonet demands ecclesiastical sociological research in order to gain an objective knowledge of pastoral realities—an indispensable pre-condition for the revision of the Codex.[88] De Echeverría stresses the need of a scientific juridical sociology, a systematic study of the causes of current law and the way it operates, without which there is no real understanding of justice or law, and he demands that a new law be planned. The sociological outlook found expression in *L'Année Canonique*.[89] As sources of information about how the Codex works in reality the author mentions: the legislation which came after the promulgation of the codex;[90] local councils and synods;[91] jurisprudence;[92] *L'Attività della S. Sede*, the *Annuario Pontificio* and similar national publications which contain data on the factual situation of the Churches; specialized studies, still few in number,[93] and the inquiries undertaken by ecclesiastical sociolo-

[86] *Ibid.*, pp. 161-3.
[87] *Estudios de Deusto* 9 (1961), pp. 267-9.
[88] *Ibid.*, p. 14.
[89] 1952; particularly G. Le Bras, *op. cit.*, "Sociologie religieuse et droit canonique," pp. 73-6.
[90] On Oriental law as a model for Latin law, see Pujol; Breydy; I. Zužek, "Trials before a Single Judge in the Eastern Canon Law," in *Orientalia Christiana Periodica* 30 (1964), pp. 510-25; Arza, p. 160, n. 5.
[91] Thus the Roman Synod is referred to by Ciprotti, *Il Codice*, p. 18; Arza, p. 160 and Pérez, p. 252, n. 16, for social legislation; Pérez, p. 240, n. 2 and J. Reed, "The Laity in Church Law," in *Theological Studies* 24 (1963), pp. 612-5 for lay law; on this point Breydy refers to the Diocesan Synod of Cologne in 1954 and to the Diocesan Synod of Münster in Westfalen in 1958; Pérez refers for economic law to the Premier Synode du Diocèse de Sherbrooke (Canada).
[92] Only the Rota publishes yearly the greater part of decisions given ten years ago; the Congregation of the Council recently published the *Thesaurus Resolutionum Sacrae Congregationis Concilii . . . in causis propositis annis 1909-1910*, tomus 168 (Rome, 1963); tome 167 appeared in 1908, the year of the reform of the curia by Pius X.
[93] For instance: L. Pérez Mier, *Sistemas de dotación de la Iglesia católica* (Salamanca, 1949); P. Winninger, *Construire des églises. Les dimensions des paroisses et les contradictions de l'apostolat dans les villes* (Paris, 1957); *ibid.*, "Les villes aux mains des vicaires," in *Revue de droit cano-*

gists.[94] Important factors in vitalizing the law are the wider recognition of customary law[95] and the drastic simplification of written law, particularly of penal law.[96]

The most urgent task of the canonists will be to "order" the Church's life according to the new norms, *i.e.,* to create a system that ensures satisfactory application and observance, and in which everyone can feel that his position is secure. Painfully little has come of Pius X's constitution *Sapienti consilio;* of the reform of the curia by which the various congregations would take on administrative functions, and the *Rota* and *Signatura* would take charge of judicial matters; of the extensive procedural law in the Code by which in principle the judge would uphold every right and sentence most of the legal offenses. The Rota—not to mention lower tribunals—deals almost exclusively with marital questions; there are never any penal sentences. Disputes are settled and penalties imposed administratively by episcopal curias and Roman congregations. In the case of wrongful treatment by a superior it is, in practice at least, impossible to go to the judge, and one car go only to a higher superior. If in practice there exists, as in the United States, a *privilegium fori* which relies on

---

nique 8 (1958), pp. 34-61; *ibid.,* "Le problème des trop petites paroisses," in *La Maison-Dieu* 57 (1959).

[94] For cxample, J. Kerkhofs, "Aspects sociologiques du sacerdoce," in *Nouvelle Revue Théologique* 82 (1960), pp. 289-99; "Vernieuwing der priesteropleiding," in *Streven* 18 (1965), pp. 318-27, with bibliography.

[95] McManus, p. 275; Örsy, *Vie,* pp. 959-61 and 963f.; *Towards,* p. 388; Kemmeren, *Hedendaagse,* pp. 368f., with reference to K. Rahner, *Das Dynamische in der Kirche,* p. 62.

[96] McManus, pp. 273 and 281f.; Bernhard, p. 140; Abbo, pp. 394f.; on the revision of the Penal Code: A. Bride, "L'évolution du droit pénal depuis le Code," in *L'Année Canonique* 2 (1953); pp. 303-21; O. Cassola, "De jure poenali Codicis canonico emendando," in *Apollinaris* 32 (1959), pp. 240-59; *ibid.,* "Natura e divisione del delitto: osservazioni de jure condendo," in *Apollinaris* 34 (1961), pp. 332-44; R. Castillo Lara, "Algunas reflexiones sobre la futura reforma del Libro VC.I.C.," in *Salesianum* 23 (1961), pp. 317-38; A. Scheuermann, "Erwägungen zur kirchlichen Strafsrechtsreform," in *Archiv für katholisches Kirchenrecht* 131 (1962), pp. 393-415; J. Baldanza, "De recognoscendo jure canonico poenali quaestiones quaedam," in *Ephemerides juris canonici* 19 (1963), pp. 93-104; and the project for Book V in Spellman.

the loyalty of Catholics not to take ecclesiastical persons or institutions to a civil court, the layman or cleric whose property is arbitrarily dealt with by the clergy, or who is deprived of a post in a Catholic institution of education or charity, or whose reputation suffers through the action of a priest, etc., is left without redress.[97]

This has been the central problem for canon lawyers during the last decades. Three Roman congresses have been working on it, in 1934,[98] 1950[99] and 1953.[100] Several publications deal with the relation between administration and the judicature,[101] the appeal

[97] McManus, p. 280.

[98] C. Bernardini, "Problemi di contenzioso amministrativo canonico specialmente secondo la giurisprudenza della Sacra Romana Rota," in *Acta congressus iuridici internationalis* Vol. IV, pp. 357–432.

[99] L. de Echeverría, "La defensa procesual del derecho en el ordenamiento canónico" and C. Lefèbvre, "Le controle juridictionnel des actes administratifs en droit canonique," in *Acta congressus internationalis juris canonici* (Rome, 1953), pp. 62–75 and 153–69.

[100] *Questioni attuali di diritto canonico* (Analecta Gregoriana, Vol. 69) (Rome, 1955): K. Mörsdorf, "De relationibus inter potestatem administrativam et iudicialem in jure canonico," pp. 399–418; S. Goyeneche, "De distinctione inter res judiciales et administrativas in jure canonico," pp. 419–34; C. Lefèbvre, "De exercitio potestatis judicialis per organa administrativa seu 'Verwaltungsgerichtsbarkeit'," pp. 435–46; C. Bernardini, "De administratione tribunalium, *i.e.,* De exercitio potestatis administrativae in ambitu tribunalium," pp. 448–55; A. Arza, "De poenis infligendis via administrativa," pp. 457–75; L. Uprimny, "De la distinción entre las funciones judicial y administrativa," pp. 477–96; reviewed by P. Huizing in *Gregorianum* 36 (1955), pp. 471-8, IV: "La potestà amministrativa e giudiziale," pp. 476-8.

[101] W. von Kienitz, *Klageinhalt und Klageänderung im Zivilprozessrecht des Codex Juris Canonici* (Munich, 1932); R. Köstler, "Kirchliche Verwaltungsberichtsbarkeit?" in *Zeitschrift des öffentlichen Rechts* 18 (1938), pp. 451f.; K. Mörsdorf, *Rechtsprechung und Verwaltung im kanonischen Recht* (Freiburg i. B., 1941); *Die Unterscheidung der Rechtswege im kanonischen Recht*, Notter Antal Emlékkönyv (Budapest, 1941), pp. 868f.; W. Brertrams, "De potestate judiciali-administrativa," in *Periodica* 34 (1945), pp. 210–30; E. Melichar, *Gerichtsbarkeit und Verwaltung im staatlichen und kanonischen Recht* (Vienna, 1948); E. Jobart, "L'exercice dans l'Eglise du pouvoir administratif et du pouvoir judiciaire," in *Rev. de droit canonique* 5 (1955), pp. 330–5; J. De Urrutia, "El campo administrativo en la actividad de la Iglesia," in *Rev. Esp. de Derecho Can.* 17 (1962), pp. 625-55; J. Noubel, "Jurisprudence de la S. Rote Romaine en matères administratives de droit canonique," in *Rev. de droit can.* 13 (1963), pp. 304–26; 14 (1964), pp. 18–31 and 339-55.

against administrative measures[102] and penal procedure.[103] The practical difficulties do not lie in the injustice or arbitrary behavior of the authorities. Once a Roman Congregation deals with a case, it will usually be dealt with impartially.[104] But a canonist who wants to help people in word and deed constantly experiences the uncertainty surrounding the judicature: he sees his right brushed aside by personal opinions;[105] he is not sure to which authority he should turn;[106] he does not know enough about jurisprudence;[107] he has no legal means to prevent his case from dragging on;[108] an appeal to distant Rome cuts him out and puts his client to considerable expense;[109] sometimes he is forced to obtain

---

[102] J. McClunn, *Administrative Recourse* (Washington, 1946); C. Cavada, *Teoría general del recurso extrajudicial* (Madrid, 1955); J. F. Noubel, "Les recours administratifs dans le code de droit canonique," in *Rev. de droit can.* 10 (1960), pp. 97–140; 11 (1961), pp. 97–121 and 227–43; I. Zužek, "The Effect of the Administrative Recourse in the Latin and Oriental Codes," in *Orientalia Christiana Periodica* 30 (1964), pp. 223–47.

[103] A. Paillot, "L'infliction de peines sous forme de précepte," in *Rev. de droit can.* 2 (1952), pp. 407–32; 3 (1953), pp. 33–49; *ibid.*, "Précepte pénal," in *Dictionnaire de droit canonique* (1958); G. Di Mattia, "Il diritto penale canonico nella giurisprudenza della S. R. Rota (Rassegna e considerazioni sulle sentenze edite e inedite dal 1936 al marzo 1960)," in *Ephemerides juris canonici* 16 (1960), pp 158–202 (continuation of P. Ciprotti, "Rassegna di giurisprudenza rotale in materia penale," in *Archivio di diritto ecclesiastico* 2 (1940), pp. 128ff., 250ff., 369ff., 583ff.,—from 1909 to 1935); J. Rietmeijer and W. Pompe, "De positie van de verdachte in de kanonieke strafprocedure," in *Annalen van het Thijmgenootschap* 50 (1962), pp. 1–42.

[104] Cf. *Gregorianum* 45 (1964), p. 604, on the *Thesaurus* of the Congregation of the Council.

[105] Breydy, pp. 149f.

[106] Bernardini, *Problemi*, p. 361.

[107] Örsy, *Vie*, pp. 959–61; *Reform*, p. 516: justice must not only be done but must be seen to be done.

[108] Hence the demand for regional tribunals: A. Caron, "Regional Tribunals," in *The Jurist* 23 (1963), pp. 423–32; Klok, p. 39; Örsy, *Vie*, p. 961.

[109] Bonet, p. 17, asks whether justice cannot be administered in the Church free of charge, and whether means can be found to ensure that all those taking part in the work of the tribunals have the right pastoral and apostolic attitude; J. Bishop, "The Advocate in Ecclesiastical Courts," in *The Jurist* 23 (1963), pp. 333-9, admits that lay lawyers would be more expensive but considers them so badly needed (because of the lack of qualified and available priests) that a special tax would be justified

justice via personal contacts as a favor when it is in fact a simple duty of authority.[110]

The new law will have to give sufficient guarantee that both subjects and authorities abide by the rules that have been laid down; it must indicate clearly which cases belong to the judicature and which to the administration, and which are the procedural stages; it must lay down which essential rules both procedures must comply with; it must see to it that the rules of jurisprudence are adequately publicized and understood; it must provide a judicial organization which can administer justice satisfactorily in a way which is expert, swift and open to all, and cover also actions involving superiors, without making the exercise of their authority impossible. This is not a light task, but it is the essential contribution of canon law to the work of Vatican Council II.

---

in order to provide some compensation for counsel in cases where the clients are poor; see pp. 336–9.

[110] Cabreros, p. 368, thinks that the more personal character of the new legislation will lead to greater security in the administration of justice. Cf. Di Mattia, p. 202.

Ivan Žužek, S.J./ *Rome, Italy*

Oriental Canon Law: Survey of Recent Developments

T he decree on the Catholic Oriental Churches of Vatican Council II was enacted principally to solve difficulties that have arisen after the publication of some sections of the Oriental Code; the difficulties originate in the close proximity of Christian Churches in the Near East. The following bibliographical survey, dealing with subjects widely discussed immediately before and during the Council, will help to clarify the criteria of the Council for forming a new Oriental Code. Moreover, it will provide assistance, one hopes, for those who will write the commentaries on the Decree on the Catholic Oriental Churches.*

I

OBJECTIONS AGAINST THE ORIENTAL CODE

When the sections of the Oriental Code dealing with marriage, ecclesiastical courts and religious were published,[1] there was little

* This article was finished on February 29, 1965, and could not go into details about the *Motu Proprio* published in *Osservatore Romano* of February 21.

[1] *Acta Apostolicae Sedis (AAS)* (1949), pp. 89–119, 5–120; (1952), pp. 67–152.

reaction on the part of Oriental Catholics. But when the schema of the section *De personis* was communicated to Melchite bishops, P. Medawar strongly protested against its implied *deminutio capitis* of the Oriental patriarchs.[2] After the promulgation of *De Personis* on June 2, 1957,[3] the position of the Melchite Church in its regard was formulated in two synods of 1958. Recourse was made to the Holy See against the new canons which enacted (1) the precedence of the cardinals over the patriarchs, (2) the curtailment of the ancient rights of the patriarchs and (3) the freedom of choosing their own rite for Oriental dissidents who became Catholics. These three points were made public by the *Mandement patriarchal*[4] of Patriarch Maximos IV.

P. Rouquette in his article "Malaise chez les catholiques de rite grec",[5] expressed the view that in some matters the attitude of the Melchites could be "a theological and disciplinary archaism, a refusal to develop and, finally, an error".[6] This phrase was a hard blow to the Melchites. P. Medawar replied by letter, which appeared also in print.[7] P. Rouquette, however, reaffirmed substantially the same view,[8] though more carefully. M. Doughty probably had P. Rouquette in mind when he wrote in 1959 that "some European commentators have seen in this malaise nothing but a spirit which looks backward, nothing but a love of archaism for the sake of community prestige . . . But the view of the Catholic Church which the leaders of the Eastern Catholic Churches

---

[2] His pamphlet "Quelques idées au sujet de l'union des Eglises" written at that time is now published in *Voix de l'Eglise en Orient* (Freiburg im Breisgau, 1962). Hereafter this book is quoted as *Voix*. Its English edition is *The Eastern Churches and Catholic Unity* (Herder-Nelson, 1963).

[3] *AAS* 1957, pp. 433–603.

[4] In *Proche-Orient Chrétien* 9 (1959), pp. 209–23. On this matter may be consulted: P. Medawar, "Quelques incidences du Synode Grec-Catholique tenu au Caire du 6. au 11 février 1958," in *Irenikon* 31 (1958), pp. 235–45; *Voix*, pp. 97–107; *Vers l'unité chrétienne* 101 (March, 1958), pp. 8–14; C. Dumont, "A propos du Synode de l'Eglise grecque catholique," in *Vers l'unité chrétienne* (September-October 1958) n. 106, pp. 1–5.

[5] In *Etudes* (June, 1958), pp. 391–4.

[6] *Ibid.*, p. 393.

[7] In *Le Lien* (1958), n. 4, pp. 4–24; in *Proche-Orient Chrétien* 8 (1958), pp. 367–70; and in *Irenikon* 31 (1958), pp. 352–7.

[8] *Etudes* (December, 1964), pp. 730–1.

keep constantly in mind is the Church not as it is now, nor even the Church as it was before the schism, but the Church as it will be when 200 million Orthodox and Monophysite Christians have returned to the unity of St. Peter".[9]

There already exists a fair literature on the ecumenical mission of Catholic Churches of the Oriental Rite in general. Clearest on this point are the words of Patriarch Maximos IV at the conference given in Düsseldorf on August 9, 1960,[10] and an article of M. Geday.[11] Geday writes that the Uniats have a tremendous mission to "open Catholic ears to the just claims of the Orthodox, their fears and their hopes",[12] to act as representatives of that part of the still dissident Church that they came from and into which they will be again absorbed after its reunion with Rome.[13] Also in agreement are the Maronites, though not in relation to the Orthodox, when they claim to act as "forerunners, witnesses and promoters"[14] of both Catholic and Oriental tradition. M. Geday says that to accomplish this "the Uniats should remain in living continuity with the Orthodox tradition, in other words they should become again substantially identical with the Orthodox (as far as possible). . . . If the Oriental Catholics do not preserve the Oriental tradition in its purity, they are no longer capable of representing the Orthodox".[15] And, it should be kept in mind that "in this field there is no room for mediocrity or worse".[16] The "archaisms" are so actual that no step forward can be made in the way of reunion without a most sincere respect for them. True, an "aggiornamento" is also needed among the Orthodox and they are trying to introduce many reforms, which, insofar as they are

[9] M. Doughty, "Rome and the Catholic East. The Misgivings of the Melchite Bishops," in *The Tablet* Vol. 213 (May 9, 1959), p. 438.

[10] Cf. *Der katholische Orient und die christliche Einheit—Unsere Okumenische Berufung.* Sonderdruck aus "Una Sancta" (Heft I, 1961); *Proche-Orient Chrétien* 10 (1960), pp. 291–302; *Voix*, pp. 20–33.

[11] M. Geday, "Uniatisme et Union," in *Le Lien* 29 (1964), n. 4, pp. 1–40.

[12] *Ibid.*, p. 37.

[13] Cf. *ibid.*, p. 36.

[14] *Antiochena* 1 (1964), n. 3, p. 5.

[15] *Op. cit.*, pp. 37–8.

[16] *Ibid.*, p. 38.

in keeping with the Catholic doctrine, the Uniats also could accept. Thus, for instance, Oriental Catholics could take into some account the proposed unification of the marriage legislation among the Orthodox.[17]

Orthodox authors, who until now have considered the Uniat Churches as "the primary obstacle to union",[18] are beginning to change their minds. H. Alivizatos, the well-known Greek Orthodox canonist, expressed in 1958 his hopes that the Uniats will make comprehensible to the Western Church certain realities not yet understood and thus become "a benediction for the suppression of divisions and the reestablishment of unity in the Church of Christ".[19]

To the above mentioned three objections against the new Oriental Code must be added others. Some of them were briefly outlined by R. Erni.[20] Others, proposed from an Orthodox point of view, were expressed by H. Alivizatos.[21] The Orthodox are filled with dismay in seeing too little consideration given in the new Code to the holy canons of the ancient councils and Fathers, while the footnotes are "inundated with decrees of the Latin Church"[22] to "make quite obvious the effort of assimilation and uniformity".[23] The explanation of this is simply that the new Oriental Code does not pretend to present the ancient Oriental

[17] Cf. *Vers l'unité chrétienne* 15 (January-February, 1962), p. 2, for the wishes expressed at the meeting on Rhodes in 1961, and G. Soare, "Impedimente la căsătorie necesitatea asigurării unei practici uniforme în toată Biserica Ortodoxa," in *Ortodoxia* 13 (1961), pp. 576–98, for a practical proposal.

[18] Cf. *Unitas* (English ed.) 11 (1959), p. 181; *Una Sancta* 21 (1964), p. 188; *Bulletin de presse* (Melchite) April 30, 1964), pp. 22–3.

[19] *Theologia* 29 1958), p. 484; cf. also E. Jungclausen, "Um die Rolle der Unierten Kirchen," in *Una Sancta* 18 (1963), pp. 184–8; F. Heyer, "Die oekumenische Sendung der Melkiten," in *Una Sancta* 19 (1964), pp. 11–24; J. Hajjar, *Les chrétiens uniates du Proche-Orient*, (Paris, 1962).

[20] R. Erni, "Das neue kirchliche Gesetzbuch für die katholischen Ostkirchen," in *Una Sancta* 15 (1960), pp. 154–65.

[21] H. Alivizatos, "Hē kōdikopoiēsis tōn hierōn kanonōn tōn Anatolikōn Ekklesiōn," in *Theologia* 29 (1958), pp. 475–96 ("The Codification of the Holy Canons of the 'Oriental Churches' "). For a summary of this article see *Proche-Orient Chrétien* 10 (1960), pp. 136–45.

[22] *Ibid.*, p. 485.

[23] *Ibid.*, p. 486.

law, but the previous discipline of Oriental Catholic Churches. This discipline, already strongly latinized in many matters, was regulated by the synods of Oriental Catholics and the decrees of the Holy See. The Uniat synods themselves were often in the past all too eager to bring their enactments into conformity with those of the Latin Church, and Rome certainly did not see any need to resist (indeed, sometimes just the opposite), as it would do today. The chief sources for the new Oriental Code were the *Corpus juris canonici* and the *Codex juris canonici*, yet neither is quoted in the footnotes of the Code.

By the promulgation of the *Decree on the Catholic Oriental Churches* the Oriental Code begins a new period of its history. Therefore, it seems well to indicate where the literature on it published until now may be found.

BIBLIOGRAPHICAL SOURCES PRIOR TO 1962

Arnold, F. "Der Codex für die Orientalische Kirche. Das Prozesrecht," in *Oestereichische Archiv für Kirchenrecht* 1 (1950), pp. 165–80.

Delchard, A. "Motu proprio *Sollicitudinem Nostram,*" in *Nouvelle Revue Théologique* 72 (1950), pp. 418–9.

Hernandez, A. S. *Iglesias de oriente* Vol. 2 (Santander: Repertorio bibliografico, 1963), pp. 447–64.

Szentirmai, A. "Legal Language of the New Canon Law of the Oriental Churches," in *The Jurist* 22 (1962), pp. 39–70, esp. pp. 39–40 (footnote 7); also in *Apollinaris* 35 (1962), p. 371–2.

Recent Articles

DeClercq, C. "La part laissée au droit particulier par les canons 16–159, 221–57, concernant les personnes en droit canonique oriental," in *Apollinaris* 35 (1962), pp. 250–8.

Faltin, D. "De legibus quibus baptizati acatholici ritui orientali adscripti tenentur," in *Apollinaris* 35 (1962), pp. 238–49.

Hajjar, J. "Quelques jalons modernes de la Codification canonique et orientale," in *Apollinaris* 35 (1962), pp. 231–7.

Mahfoud, G. "L'organisation monastique dans l'Eglise Maronite," in *Revue de droit canonique* 14 (1964), pp. 84–91.

McNicholas, T. "Matrimonial Legislation for the Oriental and Latin Churches," in *The Jurist* 22 (1962), pp. 174–204.

Oesterle, G. "De clausura monalium in Ecclesia Orientali," in *Monitor Ecclesiasticus* 88 (1963), pp. 117–30.

Pospishil, V. *Code of Oriental Canon Law: The Law on Marriage.* Chicago, 1962.

Pujol, C. "Peculiaris quaestio de forma canonica matrimonii ratione ritus," in *Periodica de re morali canonica liturgica* 51 (1962), pp. 129–66.

Zužek, I. "The Effect of the Administrative Recourse in the Latin and Oriental Codes," in *Orientalia Christiana Periodica* 30 (1964), pp. 223–47; *idem.*, "Trials before a Single Judge in the Eastern Canon Law," *ibid.*, pp. 510–25.

RECENT WORKS ON TOPICS OF HISTORICAL INTEREST

Botte, B. "Les plus anciennes collections canoniques du Patriarche Išo' narnun encore inédites," in *Apollinaris* 35 (1962), pp. 259–65.

Hafouri, G. "Les délits et les peines dans l'Eglise Syrienne d'Antioche," in *L'Orient Syrien* 8 (1963), pp. 425–52.

Zužek, I. *Kormčaja kniga: Studies on the Chief Code of Russian Canon Law.* Rome: Orientalia Christiana Analecta 168, 1964.

II

THE PROBLEM OF PRECEDENCE

This question was usually termed the problem of precedence of patriarchs over cardinals. In these terms it seemed impossible to sustain one of these most venerable institutions in the Church without offending the other. However, the recent solution of the problem by the Holy Father has gone beyond this terminology and shown once more that Christ's charity is unbounded.

Here is given a short account of the preliminaries to this solution.

Whatever one may have thought on this matter the Orthodox, knowing that we considered the chiefs of the Oriental Catholic Churches as true patriarchs, were "shocked" that we "did not treat them as a patriarch ought to be treated according to their tradition".[24] In this matter Oriental Catholics felt obliged to use every legitimate means to "prepare the house".[25] No one could have doubted the word of Patriarch Maximos IV when he declared to be acting "not through pride, as some suppose it to be, nor to seek vain honor, nor even in order to enhance our small community", but because he felt "obliged to smooth the way of

[24] T. Duprey in *Proche-Orient Chrétien* 14 (1964), p. 255.
[25] His Eminence Cardinal Lercaro in *Quotidiano* (November 14, 1964).

union and to remove obstacles".[26] Thus he wanted to reestablish the place of "apostolic sees" which "was and ought to be the first after that of the Roman pontiff, without any intermediary".[27]

Why Constantinople has second place also in the Catholic Church (for Alexandria, Antioch and Jerusalem the apostolicity seems to be certain), as stated in Can. 219 of the *Motu Proprio*: *Cleri sanctitati*, is explained in an article by O. Kerane, in a rather popular manner.[28] An interesting but debatable view is expressed by E. Zoghby. In what regards the other patriarchal Sees in the East he says that "they fulfill the conditions necessary to be true patriarchates because they are Mother-Churches; but they cannot pretend to raise themselves to the rank of the traditional patriarchates, because they *are Mother-Churches only on a local or national plan*, whereas the five patriarchates of Christian antiquity have been and continue to be the *Mother-Churches on the level of universal Christianity.* . . . On the universal scale the Roman primatial See and the four Patriarchal Sees of the East *formed the Christian Churches*, (or) *integral Christianity.*"[29]

P. Medawar and O. Kerame in almost all their writings[30] insist on the following points:

1. The precedence as enacted in ecumenical councils belongs to the ancient rights of the Oriental patriarchs.

2. The Holy See often solemnly promised to respect these rights.[31]

3. The Oriental patriarchs are direct successors of the apostles.

4. They have merited greatly by having defended Christianity in a Moslem world.

[26] *Mandement patriarcal* of 1959 in *Proche-Orient Chrétien* 9 (1959), p. 220.

[27] *Loc. cit.*

[28] O. Kerame, "Question et reponse," in *Le Lien* 28 (1963), n. 3, pp. 18–22.

[29] E. Zoghby, "En marge du concile," in *Le Lien* 29 (1964), n. 3, p. 9.

[30] Cf., *e.g., Voix*, pp. 90–1, 103.

[31] Cf. W. de Vries, *Rom und die Patriarchate des Ostens*, (Freiburg–Munich, 1963), pp. 247–60 and 285–96, for the misunderstandings in this field.

5. To honor Oriental patriarchs means to appreciate the enormous amount of Christian culture and sanctity of the East.

6. The honor given to the patriarchs will bring out more clearly the fact that the Roman pontiff is not only the patriarch of the West, but the holder of primacy over the whole Church.

7. If nobody precedes the patriarchs, except the Roman pontiff, the Orthodox will know that all their ancient rights will be respected.

8. Yet in the new Oriental Code the patriarchs appear second to cardinals, second to apostolic delegates, and to Latin bishops in the places subject to their jurisdiction. A decree of the Pontifical Commission for the Preparation of the Oriental Code concerning apostolic delegates was issued on June 23, 1958. In it the precedence of the patriarch was recognized when he is in his own territory and presides over a ceremony in his own rite.[32]

On January 12, 1962, the Central Commission of the Council accepted for discussion a project on the precedence of the patriarchs.[33] The decision was to remit the whole question to the Roman pontiff himself, but the mere fact of the acceptance of such a project had a great ecumenical echo.[34]

In March, 1963, all Catholic Oriental patriarchs became members of the Sacred Congregation for the Oriental Church.[35] C. Dumont commented on this fact saying that "the decision of John XXIII introduces into the Congregation all the Oriental Catholic patriarchs, as a group. This is to place them, in this at least, on the same level as the cardinals".[36] The Melchites in *Proche-Orient Chrétien*[37] noted the fact, but without commentary. In *Le Lien,* however, appeared a commentary written by a certain "O.K." in

---

[32] *AAS* 1958, p. 550; cf. A. Wuyts, "Nota de praecedentia patriarcharum," in *Periodica de re morali canonica liturgica* 4 (1960), pp. 489–96.

[33] Cf. *Osservatore Romano* (January 19, 1962), p. 1.

[34] Cf. *Proche-Orient Chrétien* 12 (1962), p. 52.

[35] Cf. *Osservatore Romano* (March 24, 1963), p. 2, and *Servizio Informazioni Chiesa Orientale* (March 30, 1963), where, on pp. 13-6, is reprinted the article from *Osservatore Romano*.

[36] In *Vers l'unité chrétienne* 16 (1963) March–April, nn. 3–4/151-2, p. 17.

[37] *Proche-Orient Chrétien* 13 (1963), p. 79.

which was explained in very bitter terms why this promotion of the patriarchs was for Melchites "an added bitterness".[38] The *Osservatore Romano* noted at this occasion: "It is clear that the gesture of the Roman pontiff must be understood in the light of the history and juridical importance of the figure of the patriarchs. The number of the faithful who today pertain to each patriarchate has little relevance and alone could not explain the august decision."[39]

With this the *Osservatore* proposed the view fully in keeping with what Oriental Catholics and Orthodox think, namely, that the importance of the patriarchs comes not from the number of the faithful, but from their ancient dignity and status. E. Zoghby expressed this in the following way: "The Patriarch of Moscow, who is the head of the Orthodox Church, by far the most important as regards the number of his faithful, did not hesitate to prostrate himself before Christophoros of Alexandria, when he met him some years ago, and will not hestitate to do this before each one of his colleagues of Constantinople, Antioch and Jerusalem." [40]

On October 14, 1963, at the 47th session of the Council, the Oriental patriarchs, on the insistence of Patriarch Maximos IV,[41] were seated on a special place at the left side of the altar.[42]

The situation has obviously been altered by the nomination to the cardinalate on January 25, 1965 of three patriarchs and

[38] In *Le Lien* 28 (1963), n. 3, p. 4. "O.K." seems to be the same as Latinor who wrote the article "Patriarcat et Cardinalat" in *Le Lien* 26 (1961), nn. 7–8, pp. 181–4.

[39] *Osservatore Romano* (March 24, 1963), p. 2.

[40] *Le Lien* 29 (1964), n. 3, p. 1.

[41] Cf. *Proche-Orient Chrétien* 13 (1963), pp. 329–30.

[42] Cf. *Osservatore Romano* (October 15, 1963), p. 3. In the Council of Florence the Greek prelates were on the left of the altar and facing the cardinals; cf. J. Gill, *The Council of Florence* (Cambridge, 1959), p. 107, and the interesting note in *Proche-Orient Chrétien* 13 (1963), pp. 315–6 (based on "Andrea da S. Croce," according to which the Latin Patriarch of Jerusalem was seated "between the first and the second cardinal bishop", in *Concilium Florentinum,* ed. G. Hofman, Vol. VI [Rome: Series B. Acta Latina, 1955], p. 28). *Proche-Orient Chrétien* asserts that later he was seated after all the cardinals: certainly his signature to the decree of union is after those of the cardinals.

by the *Motu proprio: Ad pupuratorum patrum* of February 11, 1965, which was published in the *Osservatore Romano* of February 21.

III
THE ANCIENT RIGHTS OF THE PATRIARCHS

In regard to patriarchs much study will be needed to determine which were their "rights and privileges . . . operative in the time of union between the East and the West",[43] in order to reestablish them in all their rights. I use the word "reestablish" with a set purpose, though the Decree on the Catholic Oriental Churches avoids it, saying only "instaurentur" in n. 9. In fact the decree itself tacitly recognizes that the *jura et privilegia* were at different times curtailed in the canon law of Oriental Catholics.[44] Writing on the new Oriental Code, C. Dumont explained why the Orientals complain about the numerous canons dealing with the rights of the patriarchs. He gives the following reasons:

1. These rights "were 'granted' rather than 'recognized' ".[45]

2. The patriarchs "were in many cases limited in the exercise of their jurisdiction by the necessity of confirmation by the Roman See".[46]

3. The Code contains "a certain number of dispositions considered discriminatory and contrary to the traditional rights and privileges of the patriarchs and patriarchates".[47]

The last distinction between patriarchs and patriarchates is noteworthy. As a matter of fact what really matters here are the rights of the patriarchates as a whole. These are considered as Churches which in the time of union between East and West enjoyed autonomy in disciplinary matters. The word "autonomy" was disliked by the Council, but what it means is recognized in

---

[43] *Decree on the Catholic Oriental Churches*, Art. 9.
[44] Cf. W. de Vries, *op. cit.*, pp. 268–85.
[45] *Vers l'unité chrétienne* 16 (March-Aprii, 1963), nn. 3–4, p. 17.
[46] *Ibid.*, p. 17–8.
[47] *Ibid.*, p. 18.

the decree. There it is said that "the patriarchs with their synods constitute the superior authority for all the affairs of the patriarchate".[48] *Proche-Orient Chrétien* wrote: "The effective recognition of the canonical autonomy of the Oriental Churches, within the limits, obviously, of the divine constitution of the Church, this is to say under the universal jurisdiction of the successor of Peter, is one of the most important preliminary conditions for all serious progress in the reconciliation of the Churches." [49] This is now achieved. After this it is not so difficult to determine the limitations of the rights of the patriarchs by different bodies (synods) existing within the patriarchate. In this regard the new Oriental Code seems to be already substantially arranged "according to the ancient traditions . . . and decrees of the ecumenical synods".[50]

To understand the discipline of the Oriental Code cf. E. Eid, *La figure juridique du patriarche* (Rome, 1962).

A few important essays appeared recently treating these topics from a canonico-historical point of view. See W. de Vries, "La S. Sede ed i patriarcati cattolici d'Oriente," in *Orientalia Christiana Periodica* 27 (1961), pp. 313–61; *idem*, "Die Entstehung der Patriarchate des Ostens und ihr Verhältnis zur päpstliche Vollgewalt," in *Scholastik* 37 (1962), pp. 341–69; the most important work of de Vries is *Rom und die Patriarchate des Ostens*, mentioned above.

OTHER WORKS

Clement, M. *L'apparition du Patriarcat dans l'Eglise*. Dissertation, Lyons: Faculty of Canon Law, 1963; reviewed in *Le Lien* 28 (1963), n. 3, pp. 30–1.

Dvornik, F. *Byzance et la primauté romaine*. Paris: Unam Sanctam 49, 1964.

Every, G. *The Byzantine Patriarchate*. London, first edition 1945, new edition 1962.

Grotz, H. *Die Hauptkirchen des Ostens*. Rome: Orientalia Christiana Analecta 169, 1964; reviewed in *Orientalia Christiana Periodica* 30 (1964), pp. 281–5, by W. de Vries.

[48] *Decree on the Catholic Oriental Churches,* Art. 9.
[49] *Proche-Orient Chrétien* 12 (1962), p. 53.
[50] *Decree on the Catholic Oriental Churches,* Art. 9.

Hageman, W. "Die rechtliche Stellung der Patriarchen von Alexandrien und Antiochen," in *Ostkirchliche Studien* 13 (1964), pp. 171–91.

Kerame, O. "Le Pape Saint Gregoire le Grand, père des Anglais et de l'Europe: sa doctrine du Patriarcat (540–604)," in *Le Lien* (1958), n. 3, pp. 24–32.

Kreilkamp, H. *The Origin of the Patriarchate of Constantinople and the First Roman Recognition of Its Patriarchal Jurisdiction.* Dissertation, Washington, D.C.: The Catholic University of America, 1963.

Lanne, D. "Eglises locales et patriarcats à l'époque des grands conciles," in *Irenikon* 34 (1961), pp. 292–321.

Ramiz, L-J. *Le pape et le patriarche.* Paris, 1964.

Siess, F. *Die Patriarchalverfassung der Unierten Kirche.* Erlangen, 1960. A dissertation reviewed in *Ostkirchliche Studien* 11 (1962), p. 372.

Zananiri, G. *Pape et Patriarche.* Paris, 1962. Reviewed in *Vers l'unité chrétienne* (1963), pp. 2–4.

With reference to the Oriental major archbishops, whose authority is almost equal to that of the patriarchs, there is an interesting essay by I. Stanculescu (Orthodox) in *Studi Teologice* 14 (1962), pp. 598–617. Among Oriental Catholics only the Ukrainian Church has such an archbishop. Cf., for example, *Servizio Informazion Chiesa Orientale,* (January 31, 1964); *Der Christliche Osten* 19 (1964), p. 12; I. Patrylo, *Figura juridica Archiepiscopi-Metropolitani Kievo-Haliciensis attentis praescriptis M.P. "Cleri sanctitati".* Rome, 1962.

IV

THE PATRIARCHS OF ANTIOCH

The much discussed question of which of the three Catholic (and two non-Catholic) "Patriarchs of Antioch" is the legitimate successor in the See, is extremely interesting from an academic point of view. I. Dalmais writes: "Can one dream that one day, more or less near, the different Patriarchs of Antioch . . . will declare solemnly that they constitute only one patriarchate administered collegially with respect to the legitimate diversity of 'nations' ".[51] C. Spiessens decided the question in favor of the

[51] I. Dalmais, "La difficile unité dans la diversité: tensions, ruptures et coexistences dans la patriarcat d'Antioche," in *L'Orient Syrien* 8 (1963), pp. 119–20.

actual Orthodox Melchite Patriarch Theodosy VI.[52] The Maronite point of view is expressed several times in *Antiochena*.[53] They propose the following points:[54]

1. In a given territory there should be only one territorial jurisdiction.

2. Where the good of a sufficient number of faithful of a different rite demands a jurisdiction proper to this rite, the jurisdiction will be only personal but always dependent on the higher jurisdiction of the same rite.

3. In the East where several jurisdictions are placed together in the same territories, the Sees will be divided among the different jurisdictions.

In practice the proposal is for a Copt patriarch in Alexandria, a Melchite in Jerusalem and a Syrian (Maronite or Syro-Catholic) in Antioch. The difficulty, however, is that many authors held that the actual Melchite patriarch, namely Maximos IV, is the real successor in the See of Antioch.[55] A unification of jurisdiction would be good especially from an ecumenical point of view. However, for the Catholics now it is extremely difficult. Here the words of M. Geday seem to be apropos: "On the Uniat level the problem is insoluble. If one maintains distinct jurisdiction one will not avoid the disagreeable impression of a badly unified East. But if one reduces the jurisdictions to unity one risks producing a monster that the authentic East will find difficult to recognize as a legitimate child. This dilemma forces us once again to place ourselves in the field of ecumenism."[56] Whatever one may think about this anomalous position of the "Patri-

---

[52] C. Spiessens, "Les patriarches d'Antioche et leur success apostolique," in *L'Orient Syrien* 7 (1962), pp. 389–434.

[53] Cf. M. Doumith, "Les Maronites dans l'histoire et le patriarcat d'Antioche," in *Antiochena* 1 (1964), n. 2, pp. 7-13, and "De l'unité de jurisdiction dans l'Eglise Orientale," *ibid.*, pp. 19–26.

[54] *Ibid.*, pp. 25-6.

[55] Cf., *e.g.*, E. Cardinale Hygin in *Unitas* (English ed.) 14 (1962), pp. 30–9; J. Nasrallah, *Chronologie des patriarches melkites d'Antioche de 1500 à 1634*, which is an excerpt from *Proche-Orient Chrétien* (1956–57) and is reviewed in *Revue des études byzantines* 21 (1963), 313–4; W. de Vries, *Rom und die Patriarchate des Ostens*, pp. 88–91.

[56] *Le Lien* 29 (1964), n. 4, p. 35.

archs of Antioch", the Council could not do more about it than
to declare that the patriarchs, "though some are later than others
in time, nevertheless all are equal by reason of the patriarchal
dignity".[57]

V

THE LATIN PATRIARCH OF JERUSALEM

Much less involved is the position of authors toward a Latin
patriarchate of Jerusalem. P. Medebielle, with a pamphlet of
1961,[58] endeavored to show that this patriarchate and the Latin
rite Catholics belong to the Near East no less than other Christian
communities living there. *Voix de l'Église en Orient*[59] seems to
be convincing in the refutation of his arguments point by point.
More moderate, yet deeper and still more convincing, is the refutation of Y. Nolet de Brauwere, though the author does not even
mention Medebielle expressly.[60]

When the Oriental patriarchs became members of the Sacred
Congregation for the Oriental Church, then "using a broad criterion, the Patriarch of Jerusalem was also included, who *ratione
territorii* depends on the Sacred Congregation for the Oriental
Church".[61] For the same reason he was seated in the Council
(from 47th session on) in the special place reserved to the Oriental patriarchs. However, he remains titular patriarch of the
Latin Church, and as such is in the same position as the patriarchs
of Venice, Lisbon, Madrid and Goa, or those Latin patriarchs of
Constantinople, Alexandria, and Antioch, whose origin dates
from the Crusades and who are now no longer mentioned in the
Annuario Pontificio (from 1964 on). Archbishop Pietro Sfair
notes that the petition to abolish the titular patriarchate of Anti-

---

[57] *Decree on the Catholic Oriental Churches*, Art. 8.
[58] Published later in 1962 in Jerusalem under the title *Le Patriarcat
latin de Jerusalem.*
[59] *Voix*, pp. 143–61.
[60] Y. Nolet de Brauwere, "L'Eglise de Terre Sainte," in *Irenikon* 36
(1963), pp. 177–203.
[61] *Osservatore Romano* (March 24, 1963), p. 2.

och, presented in 1634 by the Maronites to Pope Paul V, was now "fulfilled in the time of Paul VI, 330 years later".[62]

VI
THE JUS CONDENDUM AND THE
ANCIENT RIGHTS OF THE PATRIARCHS

Tempore unionis, i.e., for the Byzantines during the first thousand years of their existence, the regulation of ecclesiastical discipline was left entirely to each patriarchate. The interventions of Rome during this time were rare, it seems, and often, though not exclusively, confined to the use of the *jus vigilantiae,* based upon the primacy, to preserve both doctrine and morals. It is to be noted that some Oriental prelates desire a single Code for the whole Church, while others think that two distinct Codes are "a necessary guarantee against latinization".[63] There could be several distinct Oriental Codes, for instance, one for each of the five principal rites.

VII
CHANGING OF RITE FOR ORIENTAL NON-CATHOLICS

One of the most discussed points in the Council was a canon of the *Motu Proprio: Cleri sanctitati:* "Baptized non-Catholics of the Oriental rite, who are admitted into the Catholic Church, can embrace whatever rite they prefer; nevertheless it is desired that they retain their proper rite."[64]

On this subject one cannot speak about "ancient rights" of the Oriental Churches before the schism. In a few important documents before Leo XIII the Holy See expressed its wishes that the Oriental dissidents who became Catholics should retain the rite in which they were born. The encyclical letter *Orientalium dig-*

[62] This was said by Archbishop Pietro Sfair in the Council of October 19, 1964. Cf. *Antiochena* 1 (1964), n. 3, p. 25.

[63] *Proche-Orient Chrétien* 14 (1964), p. 254.

[64] *Cleri sanctitati,* Can. 11.

nitas of Leo XIII of November 30, 1894, punished with a *suspensio a divinis ipso facto incursa* "any Latin missionary whether from the secular or regular clergy, who by counsel or in any other way brings any Oriental into the Latin rite".[65] But a strong latinization continued in the Near East.[66] When canon 11 abrogated the discipline enacted in *Orientalium dignitas,* the reaction of the Melchites was very strong. P. Medewar said that this canon was "a knock-out blow delivered against the development and even against the preservation of an Oriental Church in Catholicism".[67] Patriarch Maximos IV said that the canon "authorizes the Latins to latinize",[68] *i.e.,* to accept Oriental non-Catholics into the Latin rite, but "does not authorize the Orientals to admit Occidental dissidents into their Church".[69] In fact, the Holy See never considered a converted Protestant juridically as an Oriental, if he chose an Oriental rite in some way other than by a permission from the Holy See. The above canon really "gives the impression of being based on *praestantia juris*" [70] of the Latin rite.

In the Council many Orientals did not agree with the Melchites. Those especially who saw in the Melchites' solution the abrogation of the right of an Oriental non-Catholic to choose freely any Oriental rite strongly reacted. This right was given by a decree of the Sacred Congregation for the Propagation of the Faith in 1838,[71] and this was confirmed again after *Orientalium dignitas* was issued on February 4, 1895.[72] The Maronites are all Cath-

[65] *Acta Leonis XIII,* 1894, p. 363.

[66] E. Herman in *Orientalia Christiana* 32 (1933), p. 125, stated that the above punishment was abolished by the *Codex juris canonici.*

[67] *Voix,* p. 101. For the history on latinization of Oriental rites cf. W. de Vries, *Rom und die Patriarchate des Ostens,* pp. 183–222.

[68] Cf. *Mandement patriarcal* of 1959 in *Proche-Orient Chrétien* 9 (1959), p. 221.

[69] *Ibid.,* p. 221.

[70] R. Erni, in *Una Sancta* 15 (1960), p. 156.

[71] Cf. *Collectanea* Vol. 1, n. 878.

[72] *Ibid.,* Vol. 2, n. 2, p. 315.

olics, but they insist that they are Syrians[73] and, therefore, that they have the right to accept any Syrians into the Maronite rite.[73a]

VIII

COMMUNICATIO IN SACRIS

The Decree on Ecumenism affirms that by the Eucharist "the unity of the Church is both signified and effected".[74] In 1959 C. Dumont, in answering the late Russian Orthodox Bishop Cassian, stressed the first part of this clause, excluding intercommunion in relation to the eucharist. He said that the holy eucharist "being the symbol of unity of Christians in Christ",[75] can be given only to those who are "truly and totally united among themselves by one and the same faith".[76] However, the word *efficitur* ("effected") in the above clause seems to favor those who teach that "the eucharist is not only the final expression of the unity already realized, but also a powerful means for bringing it about".[77]

In 1961 B. Schultze wrote the article "Il problema della 'communicatio in sacris' " which has been several times reprinted.[78] Schultze maintains that every baptized Christian can be admitted to the sacraments in the Catholic Church because he is "whether he likes it or not, a subject of the Church".[79] For the Catholics who wish to receive sacraments in a non-Catholic Church, he states the following principle: "The Catholic Church can always

[73] Cf. about their reaction *Antiochena* 1 (1964), no. 1, pp. 30, 42; n. 2, p. 22; n. 3, p. 2, etc.

[73a] An interesting dissertation (still unpublished) on these matters was discussed at the Lateran University in Rome in 1964: S. Mudry, *De transitu a ritu byzantino-ucraino ad ritum latinum.*

[74] *Decree on Ecumenism*, Art. 2.

[75] *Vers l'unité chrétienne* 12 (1959), n. 7, p. 57.

[76] *Ibid.*

[77] Symeon Hieromonk (Orthodox) in *Contacts* 16 (1964), p. 140.

[78] *Unitas*, (English ed.) 13 (1961), pp. 33–43; *Documentation Catholique* 43 (1961), pp. 311–20; *The Eastern Churches Quarterly* 14 (1961), pp. 197–202 (summarized); *Theologie und Glaube* (1961), Vol. 6, pp. 437–46.

[79] *Unitas* (Italian ed.) 16 (1961), p. 47.

regulate the sacraments administered outside of the Church by dissident priests, because the sacraments . . . remain its legitimate property."[80] Though somewhat criticized by K. Kappel,[81] this article had the merit of considering *communicatio in sacris,* taken in itself, as a matter of merely ecclesiastical law.[82]

The summary of all theological discussion on this matter is now given in the Decree on Ecumenism: *communicatio in sacris* depends on two main principles: "first that of the unity of the Church which ought to be expressed; and second, that of the sharing in means of grace. The expression of unity very generally forbids common worship. Grace to be obtained sometimes commends it".[83]

Patriarch Maximos IV put forward six points to show that *communicatio in sacris* among the Oriental Christians "is not only possible but also advisable".[84] These reasons are:

1. Oriental non-Catholics must be reconciled with the Catholic Church more than "converted" to it and for this "the best means"[85] is to multiply contacts.

2. They are of "absolute good faith" and the contrary is "a very rare exception".[86]

3. When there is danger of a schism severe measures are necessary "to stifle the evil in the bud",[87] but the Church is more indulgent when "Christians with no fault of theirs are born into a Christianity already split".[88]

[80] *Ibid.,* p. 46.

[81] K. Kappel, *Die gottesdientliche Gemeischaft zwische Katholiken und Nichtkatholiken Nach dem Codex juris canonici* (Winterthur, 1962), reviewed in *Una Sancta* 1964, n. 3, pp. 283–6, by Dr. J. Neuman.

[82] More profound treatment of this subject can be found in J. Neuman, *Auf Hoffnung hin,* (Meitingen, 1964). In this connection should be noted a dissertation (still unpublished) presented to the Gregorian University in Rome in 1963/64, by A. Heussinger, *"Communicatio in Sacris" und die Wiedervereinigung der Christen.*

[83] *Decree on Ecumenism,* Art. 8.

[84] *Ibid.,* Art. 15.

[85] *Voix,* p. 187.

[86] *Ibid.*

[87] *Ibid.,* p. 188.

[88] *Ibid.*

4. The current discipline of *communicatio in sacris* "is simply of ecclesiastical law"[89] as appears by the different attitudes toward it in the history of the Church.

5. *Communicatio in sacris* with Orientals is "neither weakness, nor a compromise on the part of the Catholic Church".[90]

6. The danger of scandal and indifferentism can be controlled by the bishops. "The scandal that is feared is most often exercized in the opposite way" insofar as "the Catholics, as well as the Orthodox, are more often scandalized not by intercommunion, but rather by its prohibition".[91]

Until the 16th century, after the schism of 1054, *communicatio in sacris* did not seem to be a problem. In a few cases it was explicitly permitted.[92] In the 17th century Latin missionaries in the Near East practiced an almost unlimited *communicatio in sacris* among Oriental Christians.

Recently the following studies have appeared on the activity of these missionaries:

P. Gregoriou (P. Paul Grigoriou-Garo, Editor of the journal *Katholiki), Ekēseis Katholikōn kai Orthodoxōn—Relations between Catholics and Orthodox* (Athens, 1958), 697 pp. This is the best documented study, though it adds little to the conclusions expressed in W. de Vries's "Das Problem der *communicatio in sacris cum dissidentibus* im Nahen Osten zur Zeit der Union (17 und 18 Jahrhundert)," in *Ostkirchliche Studien* 6 (1957), pp. 81-106, and "Eine Denkschrift zur Frage der *communicatio in sacris cum dissidentibus* aus dem Jahre 1721," *ibid.*, 7 (1958), pp. 253-66; A. Vuccino, "Apropos de la *communicatio*: quand catholiques et orthodoxes fraternisaient," in *Unitas* 14 (1961), pp. 357-80. Vuccino relies largely on Gregoriou. Ignatius a Seggiano, *L'opera dei Cappucini per l'unione dei Cristiani nel Vicino Oriente durante il secolo XVII* (Rome: Orientalia Christiana Analecta 163, 1962).

---

[89] *Ibid.*
[90] *Ibid.*
[91] *Ibid.*
[92] Cf. W. de Vries, *Rom und die Patriarchate des Osten*, p. 375.

An interesting study on Latin intolerance in relation to the Greeks is presented by H. Magoulias, "A Study in Roman Catholic and Greek Orthodox Relations on the Island of Cyprus between the Years A.D. 1196-1360," in *The Greek Orthodox Theological Review* 10 (1964), pp. 75-106.

All dissidents were until now considered excommunicated *in foro externo* and, therefore, deprived "of the right of assisting at the divine services".[93] Excommunication is a penalty and supposes a serious subjective sin, which may be presumed in virtue of Can. 2200, § 2 of the *Codex juris canonici*. Now, however, the presumption must follow the most solemn declaration of the Decree on Ecumenism, which states that those born in a dissident Church "cannot be accused of the sin of separation and the Catholic Church embraces them with fraternal reverence and love".[94] This is valid not only for the laity, but also for the dissident community as a whole, including the highest ranks of the hierarchy, as was most impressively demonstrated in the meeting between Pope Paul VI and the Ecumenical Patriarch Athenagoras. C. Dumont, in a short note published in 1964,[95] in stating that the former law remains untouched by the new discipline on *communicatio in sacris,* seemingly failed to see the great change in the presumption. His note is canonically unacceptable. The new presumption is the theological and canonical basis for the contemporary ecumenical movement.

The most favorably inclined toward a *communicatio in sacris* with Catholics seem to be the Russian Orthodox in Paris. This is a consequence of the teaching of N. Afanassieff in the Orthodox Institute of St. Serge. In his article "Una Sancta",[96] he proposes a reestablishment of communion between the Orthodox and the Catholic Church previous to an agreement on doctrine. He says that in this way "the renewal of the communion between the Churches will not surmount dogmatic differences, but neither

[93] *Codex iuris canonici,* Can. 2259, § 1.
[94] *Decree on Ecumenism,* Art. 3.
[95] In *Vers l'unité chrétienne* 17 (1964), p. 91.
[96] In *Irenikon* 26 (1963), pp. 436-75.

can the state of broken communion in which the two Churches find themselves surmount these differences *nor will it ever be able* to do so".[97] Hieromonk Symeon follows N. Afanassieff when he asserts that "it is an urgent necessity that divided Christians learn to live together" [98] and that "there is no better means toward this than prayer in common both around and with participation in the indivisible chalice of the sacrament of unity".[99] Also the late Bishop Cassian, the Rector of the Institute of St. Serge, as was mentioned above, noted the possibility of *communicatio in sacris.*

However, O. Clement and some other authors consider *communicatio in sacris* with Catholics still premature. Among the reasons they give, the principal one seems to be: In Orthodoxy the dogmas are connected in such a way that "one cannot admit that one is 'valid' if *all* the others are not. Dogma in particular seems inseparable from the eucharist and the spiritual life— it is the eucharist of the intelligence. An Orthodox then, it seems, has not the interior liberty to communicate in a Catholic Church, not because he doubts the validity of the sacrament . . . (this would be a false problem), but because he has not the right to regard this in *isolation*" [100] from other dogmas. But Clement still would not hold that the reception of the Eucharist by an Orthodox in the Catholic Church (and *vice versa*) constitutes a formal adherence.

IX

THE FORM IN MIXED MARRIAGES AMONG ORIENTAL CHRISTIANS

The decree *Tametsi* of the Council of Trent, requiring for a valid marriage the presence of the parish priest and two or three witnesses, had force only in those places where it was formally

[97] *Ibid.*, p. 465. Concerning Afanassieff, cf. also Herder-Korrespondenz 18 (May, 1964), n. 8, p. 393.

[98] Symeon Hieromonk, "De l'Eucharistie comme sacrement de l'unité," in *Contacts* 16 (1964), p. 140.

[99] *Ibid.*

[100] O. Clement, "Vers un dialogue avec le catholicisme," *Contacts* 16 (1964), p. 35.

promulgated. By the decree *Ne temere* of Pius X (1908) this discipline became universal in the Latin Church and was accepted in the *Codex juris canonici*. Neither of these three documents had by itself any force for marriages in which both parties were Oriental Christians. True, some Oriental Churches accepted *Tametsi* (Maronites, Italo-Greeks, Ruthenians in Zamošč, some Armenians [not all], and, probably, Malabarese), others, as the Ukrainians in Galicia, applied *Ne temere*. The great majority of Oriental Catholics, however, followed their constant practice according to which those marriages were considered valid which were "contracted before any priest, even if he is not the parish-priest".[101] Thus mixed marriages between Oriental Catholics and dissidents were valid even if contracted before a dissident priest in a dissident church.[102]

The discipline changed on May 2, 1949, when the *Motu Proprio: Crebrae allatae* became effective.[103] Canon 85, § 1 extended to all Oriental Catholics the form of marriage found in the *Codex juris canonici,* canon 1094 with the addition of two words (*ritu sacro*) which enacted that the blessing of the spouses is also necessary for the validity of the marriage. This canon caused many appeals to the Holy See because "the situation created as a consequence of it has rendered the Catholic Church odious to non-Catholics and has led to the nullity of thousands of marriages on the part of Catholic women with non-Catholic men, because in the East the celebration of the marriage must be carried out in the church of the bridegroom. All the faculties of dispensing particular cases in order to remedy such a situation were inefficacious".[104] The interventions of Oriental bishops in the Council

---

[101] Cf. *Acta et decreta concilii nationalis Armenorum. . . .* Rome (1913), p. 285.

[102] For the period before 1949 cf. A. Coussa, *Epitome praelectionum de iure ecclesiastico orientali,* Vol. 3 (Rome, 1950), pp. 212ff.; J. Marbach, *Marriage Legislation for the Catholics of the Oriental Rites in the United States and Canada,* (Washington, D.C., 1946).

[103] *AAS* (1949), pp. 89–119.

[104] These words are found in the *Osservatore Romano* (October 17, 1964), summarizing the intervention in the Council of the Patriarch of the Armenians.

during the sessions of October 15-20, 1964, were almost unanimous in requiring that the form of marriage prescribed in the *Crebrae allatae* be declared *ad liceitatem* only for mixed marriages of Orientals. The Right Rev. Ignatius Ziade, however, desired a more profound treatment of the matter and a previous accord with dissident Churches.[105] The Decree on the Catholic Oriental Churches solved the question in accordance with the wishes of the Oriental bishops.[106] However, in some countries the reaction to *Crebrae allatae* has been so strong that it will be hard now to create a common understanding among the Churches. In Egypt, for instance, there is now required from the bride an Orthodox profession of faith, which is considered a formal adherence to the Orthodox Church.

Since the Council little so far has been written on the form of mixed marriages among Oriental Christians. This question is treated rather in relation to all aspects of such marriages and all sorts of Christians.[107] Some recent Orthodox points of view were expressed in an article by P. L'Huillier in *Messager Orthodoxe*,[108] where there is given also[109] the viewpoint of the Orthodox Greek

[105] Cf. *Antiochena* 1 (1964), n. 3, p. 2.

[106] In Art. 18.

[107] The following can be noted here: C. Dumont, "Apropos de 'Marriages mixtes'," *Vers l'unité chrétienne* 17 (1964), n. 7, (165), pp. 1–6; C. Pujol, "Peculiaris quaestio de forma canonica matrimonii ratione ritus," in *Periodica de re morali canonica liturgica* 51 (1962), pp. 129–66, where there are proposed some elements *ad liceitatem* for a form in the marriages between Oriental Catholics. In this connection one may note the words of the Right Rev. M. Doumith: "If the canonical form in a mixed marriage is required *ad liceitatem* only, one cannot understand why it should be required *ad validitatem* for Catholics." Cf. *Antiochena* 1 (1964), n. 3, p. 14; R. Leclair, *La forme canonique ordinaire des marriages interrituels au Canada* (Ottawa, 1962) is a good illustration of Pujol's article; cf. also A. Coussa, "Animadversiones in Can. LXXII Trul.," in *Apollinaris* 32 (1959), pp. 170–81; L. Hofmann, "Formpflicht oder Formfreiheit der Mischehenschliessung?" in *Catholica* 18 (1964), pp. 241–57, is concerned primarily with Protestants, yet he presents many elements that apply also to Orientals.

[108] P. L'Huillier, "Le problème canonique des marriages mixtes," in *Messager Orthodoxe* 17 (1962), n. 1, pp. 39–45.

[109] *Ibid.*, p. 54; cf. also pp. 46–7.

Church of America.[110] This Church recognizes as valid only
those marriages which are celebrated before an Orthodox priest,
and in mixed marriages no obligation is imposed on the Orthodox
party to have children baptized in the Orthodox Church: the
priest only "suggests" this as suitable.[111]

[110] The viewpoint is exposed in the *Greek Orthodox Year Book*
(1956), pp. 98–100.

[111] For consultation on this matter: J. Cotsonis, "Das kanonische Recht,
wie es in der Kirche von Griechenland angewandt wird," in *Kyrios* 4
(1964), pp. 203–4; S. Nanakos, *"To hierapostolikon ergon eis tous
miktous gamous,"* in *Thessaloniki* (1960); N. Patrinacos, "The Sacramental Character of Marriage," in *The Greek Orthodox Theological
Review* 1 (1954), pp. 118–32; C. Vogel, "La législation actuelle sur
les fiancailles, le mariage et le divorce dans le royaume de Grèce," in
Istina (1961–62), n. 2, pp. 151–82.

PART III

DO-C DOCUMENTATION
CONCILIUM

DIRECTOR: Leo Alting von Geusau
Groningen, Netherlands

ASS'T DIRECTOR: M.-J. Le Guillou, O.P.
Boulogne-sur-Seine, France

René Laurentin/*Evry-Petit-Bourg, France*

The Virgin Mary in the Constitution on the Church

Three events have combined to create new interest in the Virgin Mary today: the activities of Vatican Council II which led to the promulgation of a text on "The Blessed Virgin Mary, Mother of God, in the Mystery of Christ and the Church" (chapter 8 of the Constitution on the Church) on November 21, 1964; the proclamation by Paul VI, of Mary as "Mother of the Church" supplemented by additional discourses; and finally the double "Mariological and Marian" Congress which took place at Santo Domingo, March 17–25, 1965.

I have been asked to contribute an analysis of the various tendencies contained in these events, and must therefore begin by placing the question and the events in their true perspective.

The questions that have arisen in connection with the Virgin Mary are but a particular aspect of that general problem created by the attempt to harmonize what may be briefly described as the post-Tridentine development with that of Vatican Council II.

There has been a new and prodigious development of mariology and Marian piety since the beginning of the 17th century. We know the positive contribution and basic authenticity of this development. Somehow it shows three special features: it was exclusively Latin, it was partly conditioned by anti-Protestant controversies, and it became highly specialized. These features tended to create a gap between theology and mariology, between sectors of the Church's life which were exclusively "Marian" and others which, through reaction or in order to maintain a balance, were not "Marian" at all. Hence a certain dissociation and tension developed within the Catholic Church. We should not exaggerate these difficulties and not overstress the "introverted" character of the Marian movement. This movement reached its highest peak during the 19th century.

But while the Marian movement thus reached its climax and achieved official recognition, a whole series of other movements have arisen in the Church during these last thirty years: biblical, ecclesiological, missionary, liturgical and ecumenical. Started, not without difficulties, by some pioneers, all these movements gained recognition and tended in the same direction. Proceeding from the same need to return to the sources, they sought to bring theory into line with practical life, to create a greater openness for dialogue and contemporary problems, and to redress the balance after the excesses of the Counter-Reformation. The result was a theoretical and practical reassessment in every field.

A general revision was bound to affect mariology, too. But it could hardly be done without inviting defensive reactions. Would this return to the Bible not mean a return to an elementary mariology? Would this search for Mary's place within the Church not lead to a flattening out of her exceptional privileges? Would the revaluation of the liturgy not lead to a devaluation of private devotions?[1] Lastly, would the ecumenical dialogue not have a corrosive influence on Marian theology and piety? Hence there was some apprehension, some reticence, and sometimes even some anxiety. As the scholastics said: "The birth of one thing is the death of another" (*generatio unius corruptio alterius*). The regeneration which was being pursued was felt by certain mari-

---

[1] As recently as 1958 a theologian published one of the most open-minded and best documented works on Mary, Mother of the Redemption, with an important section devoted to Marian piety. These pages did not mention the liturgy once, a simple oversight due to the climate of the period. It was only a few months before the promulgation of November 21, 1964, that mention of the liturgy was introduced into the conciliar schema, in n. 67.

ologists more as "corruption" than as "generation"; they were more aware of the relegation of certain formulae and perspectives to a secondary place than of constructive revaluation.[2]

At the beginning of the Council these reactions were still instinctive, and not fully understood. Neither in the centers of Marian preoccupation nor elsewhere were people fully aware of the problem.[3] They did not yet see where all this would lead, namely to a harmonious synthesis richer than the old one, but differently conceived. It was, indeed, a matter of harmonizing what was excellent in the Marian movement—that vital movement toward the Mother of God which has been a constant element in the Church's life since Christian antiquity—and the unalterable demands which converged in the Council's work.

1. *The Conciliar Text "De Beata Virgine"*

On October 29, 1963, the members of the Council were almost equally divided on whether the Schema on the Blessed Virgin Mary should be incorporated in that on the Church (1114 votes versus 1074). Exactly a year later, on October 29, 1964, the same assembly almost unanimously approved the text we have now (2080 *placet* versus 10 *non placet*). How did it happen? Not by a frontal attack but by disentangling the many points held in common. For Catholics, Mary as the Mother of God, Virgin, immaculately conceived and established "with soul and body in the glory of Christ", is a clearly defined dogma.

An intuitive groping toward unanimity profited by keeping the conciliar text within the boundaries marked by tendencies which Catholics debate among themselves, whether in theology or exe-

[2] The whole problem is dealt with *ex professo* by R. Laurentin, in *La Vierge au Concile* (Lethielleux: Paris, 1965), Chap. 2, "Requêtes conciliaires" (conciliar requests), pp. 51–75.

[3] This is why I thought it necessary to write, after the rumor of difficulties at the end of the first session, another book to encourage this growing awareness, *La Question mariale* (Paris, Les éd. du Seuil, 1963). This emergency operation was bound to provoke reactions, in spite of the tact and moderation applied, since the question was obviously going to be proposed. Any examination of conscience implies some suffering.

gesis. Nevertheless, it did not lead to a mediocre and platitudinous common denominator, but rather to a reaffirmation of what is essential (yet sometimes ignored [4]), particularly the theology of the Fathers: on Eve and Mary (Arts. 56 and 63), on the ecclesial function of the faith and of the *Theotokos* (God-bearer) in the Incarnation,[5] and on Mary as "type of the Church" (Arts. 63 and 64).

This overwhelming agreement could not have been achieved by a hodgepodge of prefabricated formulae. The wish of the fathers of the Council as well as the whole work of conciliar reform demanded that the formulation take due account of today's appreciation of the Bible, the Fathers of the Church, ecclesiology, the theology of salvation history (one section of the chapters of the Constitution mentions this in the title), ecumenism and liturgy. A text ignoring these demands would never have achieved such wide support. New needs required a fresh assessment and formulation of the Church's teaching on Mary. The conciliar text, therefore, presents the classical doctrine as it is found in the encyclicals but in a language closer to the sources and stripped of many accidental details too obviously related to a particular place, temperament or period. The essentials—the dogmatic teaching of salvation and its concrete values—stand out the better for it. If, then, the conciliar text does not say anything "new", which in any case was not its purpose, it *does* give what one could expect of a conciliar Constitution in this delicate situation:

1. It protects the essential truths as a whole.

2. By the same token it has eased much unrest and suspicion and restored on the psychological level the unity which for a moment was threatened. And so it made possible the pursuit of peaceful solutions to the problems.

---

[4] The word "ignored" does not seem abusive here. One of the papers circulated at the time of the famous vote, and carefully summarized in *Civiltà Cattolica* 114 (1963), IV, p. 531, said in so many words: "The idea of those who see in Mary the figure of the Church is totally new, is not according to Tradition, and was invented a few years ago."

[5] Arts. 53, 56, 63–5, where the patristic theme is mentioned: "She conceived in mind before she conceived in the body."

3. For this purpose it contains certain indications, instances and suggestions that should encourage pastoral workers and theologians to work seriously toward fuller authenticity.

For more details about the text, its history, and how the work should develop I refer to my book *La Vierge au Concile* (The Virgin at the Council).[6] This article can deal only with the main lines.

2. *Mater Ecclesiae: Mother of the Church*

It was the pope's wish to round off the conciliar Constitution by proclaiming Mary "Mother of the Church" in his closing address at the end of the third session, on November 21, 1964.

Paul VI saw in this title the means of integrating Mary into the Church while at the same time showing her superior position. As Cardinal Montini he had already advocated this formula and this teaching when he intervened in the debate of December 5, 1962. Supporting Cardinal Suenens (December 4), he declared: "I approve that the Blessed Virgin be honored as Mother of the Church."[7] Since then he made increasing use of this title, on August 15, November 14 and December 4, 1963, May 27, October 11 and November 18, 1964.[8]

On this last occasion, during an address given at the general Wednesday audience, he announced that he would make this proclamation on November 21. He did not say where but at that time the speech was drafted in Italian so that it could be delivered before the general public at the basilica of St. Mary Major. At the last moment it was translated into Latin and joined to the closing speech of the session. This explains its length and why it is interesting to compare the differences between the two texts.

The event has raised many questions:

1. Why did the Pope Paul make this declaration? There were many petitions, and the Polish hierarchy, intervening in August

[6] Laurentin, *La Vierge au Concile, op. cit.*
[7] *Ibid.*, p. 11.
[8] *Ibid.*, pp. 172–5, documented note on *Mater Ecclesiae* in tradition and in the documents related to the last popes.

1964, even wanted a definition, and it is rumored that a discreetly conducted petition during the session contained about five hundred signatures. These petitions confirmed the Pope in his conviction. But it was not simply these influences and his personal sentiment that moved Paul VI: he intended to make this declaration in virtue of his magisterium, after careful thought.

2. What, then, is the theological force of his statement? It is not a *definition* but a *declaration*. The closest resemblance is to Pius XII's proclamation of Mary's Queenship in 1954. The latter also gave rise to the institution of a feast in the universal liturgy of the Church, but the circumstances were not so solemn since the declaration of Paul VI was made to the Ecumenical Council.

3. Some have maintained that there was a certain opposition between the Pope and the Council. It has been emphasized that the Council had voted for certain amendments which eliminated this title formally as not sufficiently "traditional" and inopportune from an ecumenical point of view.

The word "opposition" is altogether wrong. There were here two complementary attitudes toward a title which was complex, open to various interpretations, some good, others not. The Council had to try to obtain unanimity as quickly as possible and preferred not to hold on to a title that was ambiguous and controversial although they recognized that "it was theologically admissible" and that it expressed a teaching which was certain, namely, Mary's spiritual motherhood.

Paul VI, who is free to exercise his authority without depending on such conditions, preferred to take another line. He used the title but avoided all ambiguity, and he did this with the utmost care. He restricted the meaning in order to avoid any valid objections and controversial interpretations:

(a) He insists that Mary is within the Church. "She is," he said at the beginning, quoting Rupert of Deutz, "the greater part, the better part, the principal part, the chosen part of the Church." He repeats several times that Mary is within the Church: *in Eccle-*

sia, in the Church, and within the Christian people: *in christiano populo.*[9]

(b) He maintains the balance in the use of the title by adding such complementary expressions as "our sister by the bond of nature", which he had already used on November 11, 1963, and May 7, 1964.

(c) He insists on circumscribing the title in the very sense Cardinal Frings had asked for, and did this three times by repeating: Mother of all the faithful and pastors, *i.e.,* the Church, (*Mater fidelium et pastorum omnium, scl. Ecclesiae; omnium fidelium et pastorum seu Ecclesiae matrem; mater fidelium et pastorum, id est Ecclesia.*[10]

The two words "faithful" and "pastors", which are repeated in these three texts, refer to the Church militant: the faithful, indeed, are those who live in the situation of "faith" and not of "vision". This means, in a more concrete and felicitous expression, "mother of the Church militant" which I had suggested in order to avoid such scholastic discussions as "Is Mary mother of the angels?" or, "What is Mary's maternal function toward those who are already in that glory where God is in all?"

Careful restriction of the term by Paul VI keeps the title within the sense of the conciliar Constitution. The Constitution says that "Mary is the mother of mankind, particularly the faithful". Paul VI only mentions the faithful, and does not extend Mary's motherhood more explicitly to all men. The Pope, therefore, did not intend to introduce a doctrinal innovation, but used a relatively new formula to give full expression to a very traditional doctrine. He insisted on this in his speech of November 21 and afterward.

He particularly wanted to bring together within one basic con-

[9] *Ibid.,* pp. 39–40.

[10] This last text adds the distinction that Christ "as soon as he assumed human nature joined his Mystical Body to himself as the head". This statement, somewhat new in form, must not be interpreted as opposed to the common doctrine according to which the Mystical Body was constituted at Pentecost by the sending of the Spirit, the soul of the Church (John 7, 39). At the time of the Annunciation, the Mystical Body consisted, so it seems to me, only of its first two members, Christ as the Head and the Virgin Mary, as redeemed in anticipation (see *ibid.,* p. 43).

cept Mary's function toward Christ and her function toward all men: in both cases it is the function of motherhood. By the same token he wanted to underline the "communal aspect" of this spiritual motherhood.[11] Mary is not merely the mother of individuals, but of the community.

He saw in this title the means to bring together in a formula of lapidary brevity both the somehow constitutive superior position of God's mother with regard to the rest of the Church and the living relationship she has with regard to all on a universal level. He wanted to react against interpretations that would bring Mary down to the level of the other members of the Church.

Lastly, he also wanted to meet in this way a certain devotional demand which likes to multiply the titles of the Virgin and which had for ten years marked time:

"We hope," he wrote, "that the promulgation of the Constitution on the Church, reinforced by the proclamation of Mary as Mother of the Church, that is, of all the faithful and pastors, will encourage the Christian people to approach the Blessed Virgin with more confidence and fervor."

4. Has this title "Mother of the Church" created a fresh obstacle for ecumenism?

It can hardly be denied that weighty ecumenical arguments militated against the use of this title (they were mentioned explicitly by the theological commission). Nor can it be denied that observers, particularly Protestants, were painfully surprised by this proclamation, the more so since, by being present at this Marian gesture, they felt themselves somewhat compromised. The decision provoked a certain stiffening of attitudes.[12]

The Protestants approach the Virgin as *member* and *type* of

[11] Paul VI said this explicitly in his speech of February 12, 1965, quoting J. Galot, in *Nouvelle Revue Théologique* (Dec., 1964), pp. 1180–1; cf. *Osservatore Romano*, of Feb. 3, 1965.

[12] This reason seems to have played a part in, for instance, the decision made by the Reformed Synod of Nantes, May 4, 1965, admitting women pastors. Fr. Boyer, S.S., had asked the Synod not to make this decision so as not to create a new obstacle to reunion. But the idea that each communion should decide (as seemed to be done by the Catholic Church) according to its own nature, prevailed.

the Church. But, however we explain the concept of Mother of the Church, they see in it the abrupt erection of a new wall, and this hardens their conviction that Catholic teaching on the Virgin cannot be assimilated and that it remains a source of painful surprises constantly renewed.

Nevertheless, as explained by Paul VI, this title does not really add any new difficulty as was the case with the dogmas of the Immaculate Conception or the Assumption, and the promulgation of the title of *Mediatrix* (which Paul VI has never used) would have had a much more negative effect.

Here the Pope found himself confronted by a dilemma: a minority of Council members, rather nervous about the innovations of the Council and about a seeming break with the style of Marian piety of the last two centuries, wanted him to do something that would recall the style and Marian devotion of Pius XII and his predecessors: the solemn proclamation of a great and new title. Paul VI could not reassure and rally this section of Catholic opinion without in some way alienating non-Catholic Christians.

He chose to act in a way that would strengthen internal unity by reassuring the conservative wing rather than leaving it alone, in order to facilitate progress toward reunion. He was anxious nevertheless to soften these inconveniences, and if possible to eliminate them as far as possible by means of explanations and additional developments. That was the point of the last section of his speech. The glamour of the proclamation and the emotional atmosphere pushed this part into the background, and yet Paul VI attached great importance to it. In it he underlined a series of themes up till now little used by the papal magisterium: evangelical themes that were dear to Luther and which have kept a place of honor in large sections of the Protestant faith, *e.g.,* the Virgin of the *Magnificat,* her exemplary faith and humility, the christocentric vision, the *one and only Mediator,* the "relative" function of the Mother of God. It is not exaggerating to say that he insisted on all this, since, only here, he uses the word *praesertim* (above all):

"Above all we want to make it abundantly clear that Mary, the humble servant of the Lord, is wholly related [13] to God and to Christ, our one and only mediator and redeemer . . . that the true nature and purpose of the veneration of Mary should be clarified . . . which . . . far from being an end in itself is, on the contrary, a means which is essentially meant to guide souls toward Christ. . . ."

Some Protestants were aware of the importance of this declaration for ecumenism.[14]

3. Other Public Utterances of Paul VI

Since that date Paul VI has repeatedly spoken in the same sense on several occasions, two of which were particularly significant.

There is first of all the statement in which the Pope corrected some unfortunate ways of speaking about Mary's mercy (used since the 15th century):

"There are some simple souls who believe Mary to be more merciful than our Lord. A rather childish way of thinking then leads one to say that the Lord is more severe than she; and then it is believed, *and* said, that unless we have recourse to the Mother of God the Lord will punish us. Mary certainly has an eminent function of intercession, but the Lord remains nevertheless the source of all goodness. Christ is the sole mediator, the sole source of grace. Whatever Mary has she owes to Christ. She is the "mother of divine grace" because she receives this grace from the Lord." [15]

An exhortation, given February 2, for the Mariological Congress of Santo Domingo, emphasizes the same point:

[13] This formula is an implicit quotation of Grignon de Montfort. It is evident in the Italian text: "tutta relativa a Dio" (*Traité de la vraie dévotion*, Art. 225). It is somewhat blunted in the official Latin text: "Mariam . . . ad Deum . . . totam spectare." I recall that this part of the speech was meant to be delivered at S. Maria Majore in the afternoon of November 21. It was incorporated in the closing speech after a decision which was, it seems, taken only on the eve of that date. The Latin translation was therefore made hurriedly and finished only at the last minute. Hence the importance of the slight differences in formulation between the Latin and the original Italian, and here it is particularly important.

[14] G. Richard-Molard, *L'hiver de Vatican II* (Paris, 1965), pp. 160–1.

[15] Sermon preached at Castel-Gandolfo on August 15, 1964; see *Osservatore Romano* (August 17–18, 1964).

"You should concentrate on a deeper understanding and love of the mysteries of Mary rather than on theological extensions which are questionable and lead to division rather than union. . . . You must restrain . . . unbalanced and not very enlightened sentimentalities. . . . You should encourage a serious and living devotion . . . which moves within the great coherent framework of the liturgy." [16]

In short, the line indicated by Paul VI may be said to consist in the maintenance, vitality, purity, and improved orientation of Catholic piety toward the Blessed Virgin.

4. *The Congress of Santo Domingo (March 17–25, 1965)*

Paul VI steered the Mariological Congress at Santo Domingo in the direction of balance and synthesis. He himself decided upon the place in the spring of 1964. At first he intended to go there himself and then to visit both Americas via the gateway of Christopher Columbus to the New World, but changed his plans. Today we understand why. He approved the theme for the Congress which was the Virgin Mary and the Scriptures. A theme suited to a dialogue between theologians and biblical scholars and corresponding to the schema on revelation, it would help to bring Marian doctrine and piety back to the essentials. The theme would also be ecumenical since the Bible is the source that we have in common with other Christians.

The Ecumenical Aspect. It was Paul VI's personal wish that "the still separated brethren should be present" and he welcomed this presence with "the greatest sympathy and the utmost respect".[17]

In style and orientation the plan was very new for a Marian Congress. Its novelty caused a certain embarrassment and some hesitation, and Paul's wish was fulfilled only barely, and somewhat symbolically. One single non-Catholic Christian took part in the theological dialogue at Santo Domingo. He was the young

---

[16] *Osservatore Romano* (Feb. 3, 1965); cf. *Documentation Catholique* 62 (1965), p. 393.

[17] Speech of March 17, 1965; cf. *Osservatore Romano*, (March 18, 1965).

Lutheran Pastor Kunneth whose father was one of the heroes of moral resistance under Hitler, and whose devotion to Mary is rather exceptional in Lutheran circles. The Anglican Bishop of Puerto Rico was expected for the end of the *Marian* Congress (which followed the *Mariological* Congress). However, I had to leave then and do not know whether the bishop did actually come. In the history of mariological congresses this rather limited presence may be taken as a preamble to ecumenism.

Mariologists and Biblical Scholars. The main object of the Congress was to bring about an effective confrontation of biblical scholars and mariologists. This, again, was something new, a kind of antidote to the closed atmosphere of certain types of mariology.

In spite of the work done over the last twelve years by many biblical scholars (particularly by Benoît, Feuillet, Lyonnet, Cazelles and Rigaux, who were at the Congress) in bringing out the scriptural data on the Blessed Virgin, and the corresponding work done by some mariologists in taking the literal meaning of the Bible seriously and giving it pride of place, there was no real *rapprochement*. The distance between (a) the attempts at proving that the mystery of the Annunciation "established Mary in the hypostatic order", or even that she is *causa Dei;* (b) the biblical studies which tried to render with scrupulous precision the literal meaning of the text as meant by the biblical author in the framework of his literary genre, remained as great as ever. The biblical scholars felt that they were not complementing the other point of view, but rather completely outside it.

One side was mainly concerned with scientific investigation, and proceeded with that disinterestedness such work requires; the other side was mainly preoccupied with a biblical justification of formulae used by papal encyclicals or mariological textbooks.

The main point of difference was clearly the relationship between the magisterium and exegesis. Of course, nobody doubted either the authority of the magisterium or the need of a scientific approach to the sacred text. But while one side tried to stress the authenticity of this scientific work, the other tried to restrict the magisterial limits within which such work could be allowed. This was the only issue where a certain tension was unavoidable, though the discussion remained surprisingly courteous. The members of the Congress instinctively adopted the tactics and spirit of the Council: to avoid the points of open conflict and seek out the points of agreement. And so the Congress could reach some commonly agreed conclusions, thanks to the mediating efforts of Msgr. Philips. The conclusions contained some very generous principles and the wish that constructive collaboration should prolong the first dialogue. It seems clear that the collaboration will be protracted. It was important to establish the principle of collaboration at this meeting, and thus the apprehensions of many on both sides found some reassurance.

The Papal Legate's Address (March 21). The Papal Legate, Cardinal Silva of Santiago, Chile, closed the Mariological Congress with an address that attracted a great deal of attention. The conclusions of this address are in line with the text of Vatican Council II and Pope Paul's address, and indicate a more profound commitment than the conclusions reached by the Congress itself, as a few quotations will show.[18]

The cardinal formally encouraged open-minded research in matters of exegesis as in matters of Marian theology, with full awareness of the difficulties:

"Let it not be said that this service of thought is something which descends exclusively from above. The Church is a community in which the Holy Spirit moves not only the hierarchy but also the laity. Sacred science is therefore bound to consider the phenomena of its life. . . . The Church's life and practice will always be a primary criterion in the discernment of the faith . . . yet, discernment is necessary, because all facts in the life of the Church, even relatively frequent ones, are not necessarily and from every point of view the fruit of such a divine action. . . . Certain peculiarities sometimes weaken the authentic and universal content of the faith. Theology has a double function: it must dis-

---

[18] I feel I have to deal more extensively with this speech which was not completely published. Part of it may be found in *Infor. Cathol. Intern.* 239 (May 1, 1965), pp. 26–8.

cern the truth always and in all its parts. . . . Then, in case of deviation, it must discover the marrow of truth which always exists in any error and makes it attractive. Thus we discover the way to a composite balance. . . . The way is hard and humanly speaking impossible. But the Lord gave his Church an instrument for this balance, the magisterium which he has entrusted to the college of apostles and Peter."

On the Virgin Mary herself and the veneration which is her due, the legate firmly underlined the norms laid down by the conciliar Constitution:

"We must remain aware of the fact that the greatness of the Mother of God is a gratuitous gift of God."

"We must show how the influence of Mary "favors the immediate union of the faithful with Christ" (Art. 60).

We must show how "the gifts and privileges of Mary always refer to Christ, the source of all truth, holiness and piety" (Art. 67).

We must always "carefully avoid all that, in word or in deed, may mislead our separated brethren or anyone else insofar as the true teaching of the Church is concerned" (Art. 67).

Continuing in the same vein, the cardinal developed the teaching of Paul VI, particularly the principle he laid down in his address of November 21, 1964: "The understanding of the true Catholic doctrine on Mary will always be a key to the right understanding of the mystery of the Church. . . ." The legate drew some vital consequences, unafraid of touching on such prickly questions as the institution of the Church:

"Mary did not and does not belong to the hierarchical priesthood. Her function is of another order . . . but she achieved a remarkable balance between this official function of hers and the way in which she personally responded to it in grace and love. . . . Mary has shown how impossible it is for people with ecclesial functions to give the service demanded without holiness. *If so often it is necessary to defend the institutional aspects of the Church, it is precisely because this defence is made necessary through lack of holiness.*"

The legate treated of the problems of Schema 13 in the same light. So, for instance, with regard to the Church's attitude toward the world:

"Mary cooperated in the incarnation of the Word, in what one might call the limitation of the Word. For the Word, by taking on matter, voluntarily accepted certain limits, and not only the limits of time and space, which are inherent in the vast expanse of the cosmos, but the whole gamut of human limitations implied in the vital social environment within which his life had to unfold itself. Some members of the Church sometimes refuse to accept this law of incarnation or limitation. . . . But Mary teaches us differently: she teaches that we should respect God's work in material conditions, and accept the Spirit in its incarnate form. . . . In the Blessed Virgin the Church learns to love the concrete and the limited: a basic antidote to pride."

Finally, Cardinal Silva used the situation of Mary at the Annunciation to throw light on the situation of the Church in this world:

"Mary's mission came from on high. It was not her own decision, but she was unexpectedly faced with a perspective which was beyond her and which, in a purely normal way, provoked the reaction: 'But can this be?' (Luke 1, 34). It is the same with the mission of the Church and the hierarchy; they are constantly faced with the unexpected. It is impossible to plan for everything. God's hour is always mysterious, as it was for Mary. Hence the obligation to explore the signs of the times in order to find there the indications that mark God's hour. That is why, however divine the origin of her mission, Mary remained always humble; but this humility did not compromise her efficacy. On the contrary, the whole edifice of salvation is based on materially insignificant facts."

The Pastoral Commission for Latin America. A commission composed of American theologians was given the task of surveying the future of pastoral work. One of the aims of the Marian Congress concerned Latin America, where it took place. The idea was to start from Marian piety, always so very much alive in those countries, in order to infuse new life into a Catholicism which, in certain places, shows an old and cracked surface. Its first conclusion was to endorse the authenticity of American Marian piety, lock, stock and barrel, but to accept the need for a revaluation. This piety remains, in various degrees, too sentimental, too "self-interested" and too little based on doctrine. It requires a major catechetical effort. Lastly, this piety shows too little commitment. It should lead to a demand for action in evangelization and urgent social needs. Lack of time prevented the passage of practical resolutions.[19]

At the initiative of the nuncio, Msgr. Clarizio, the Congress achieved one realistic and symbolic result. A village was founded in the shadow of the cathedral of Altagracia, the oldest Marian place of pilgrimage in Latin America, in order to relieve the housing crisis which is so serious in that island. Some criticized this initiative because the new cathedral is neither finished nor paid for. This sets one wondering. It is a typical issue for this country where the social question is serious and fundamental. Through the efforts of those who serve her, the Virgin of "Nazareth" (the name of the village) has provided new lodgings for some young families of Santo Domingo.

Conclusion

The facts and texts mentioned mark one step on the way toward a solution of the problem stated earlier: how to reconcile the movement of Marian piety (which tended to become an individualistic concern in certain circles) with the demands of the *aggiornamento* influencing every facet of the Church's life, both doctrinal and practical.

The editors of Documentation Concilium have asked me to go into further detail here, but that is not easy without making a choice. Indeed, the events I have outlined here provoked two different sets of reactions, two extreme positions among Catholics:

[19] The Acta of the Congress will be published by the Academia Mariana (Rome, Via Merulana 124) under the efficient editorship of its president, Fr. C. Balic.

One group clings to the "advances" made in the conciliar text, and insists on the universal motherhood of Mary, the emphasis the text places on this teaching, the use of the title "mediatrix" and the proclamation of Mary as "Mother of the Church". They seize upon these elements to satisfy certain "Mario-centric" tendencies, and play down the ecumenical problem in this matter. They dream of a new solemn Marian event at the end of the Council, and basically, of a consecration of the world to Mary according to the message of Fatima. A discreet but efficient movement is being organized on these lines.

The other group concentrates on the corrections which the text seems to contain rather than on its positive content. They consider the proclamation of *Mater Ecclesiae* a concession with regrettable consequences for the doctrinal orientation of mariology and for ecumenism.

Nevertheless, there is some *rapprochement* between the two tendencies. The renewal of theology progresses by way of slow osmosis. Since the promulgation of the Constitution the climate has been favorable for a dialogue between the various tendencies in mariology. A better sense of proportion seems to make headway between essential sources and recent traditions, between dogmas and personal preferences, between essential truths and accessory ones, between *the* Revelation and private revelations, and between liturgy and private devotions.

But we are not yet at the end of the road. Certain defense reactions still paralyze the renewal; some depreciation in practice and some ways of putting the Virgin Mary "in brackets" provoke mistrust, and this mistrust is mutual.

There is much work to be done, theologically and pastorally. In theology it is a matter of extending communion in what is essential to the whole of the Church, East and West. This presupposes a vast amount of work to be done on the sources and in the right direction. The results will be: an acceptance of complementary values, the relative assessment of particular tendencies, the widening of much that is too narrow, a correction of deviations which exist here and there. The true place of the Virgin, so fruitful in

Christian doctrine, must be found. This doctrine, like the rest of theology, must be given its true character, because theology is a doctrine drawn from the sources, meant to be lived (not just speculated upon), an organic doctrine where various truths have a certain hierarchy according to their relation to God and salvation, as the decree on ecumenism asserted.

Piety should never abbreviate doctrine. Devotion to the Blessed Virgin must be inspired by the goal of unity and efficacy in the pursuit of salvation. This demands less a multiplication of purely and specifically Marian activities than the recognition of Mary's true place in all Christian activity. The *Theotokos* has a universal function in the Church. She is not a separate section, apart from Christian doctrine and Christian life (although she may be legitimately the object of some special activity). But the label "Marian" and her prestige have been so exploited that Mary is the loser. We must remedy this lack of proportion seen in the multiplicity of specialized Marian institutions that are losing vigor, and the neglect of the Virgin in other institutions, sometimes called "Non-Marian". The Council encourages this attempt at adjustment and *aggiornamento*. It gives us a glimpse of the end of the road, whose meanderings we cannot yet trace: the communion of all in one renewed doctrine and piety, where the Virgin, no longer pulled in conflicting directions, will be restored to that universal and unifying place which is hers in the Church, a place where her presence will stimulate Christian demands and Christian initiative, a presence whose whole purpose is to lead us to the fullness of Christ.

PART IV

CHRONICLE OF THE
LIVING CHURCH

**IN COLLABORATION WITH
KATHOLIEK ARCHIEF**
Amersfoort, Netherlands

Arnulf Camps, O.F.M./*Nijmegen, Netherlands*

Christian Corridors to Japan: A Case-study on Pre-evangelization

For several years specialists in Western Europe have been active in the field of catechetical renewal. In this context the word "pre-evangelization" has been used many times with a variety of meanings. Through the studies of Father D. Grasso, S.J. and his disciple, Father A.M. Nebrada, S.J., an acceptable clarification has now been reached. The "homily" stands for the preaching to adult Christians; the "catechesis" introduces into the truths of the faith those who in principle resolve to become Christians; the "kerygma" intends to bring about this fundamental choice for Christ; "pre-evangelization" is a stage preceding the fundamental acceptance of Christ.

More information and literature on this subject is to be found in Nebrada's book, *Jalones para una preevangelización en Japon* (Estella, 1964). By way of exclusion, pre-evangelization thus becomes a first stage in missionary work, but the question remains: which is the exact and positive meaning? Nebrada describes it: to start from the hearer and to demonstrate a respectful attention to the spiritual situation of the non-Christian (p. 70); or, the patient attitude of a missionary who tries to discover the stepping stones

existing in the religion of the non-Christian in order to open his
heart and mind for the first preaching of Christ (p.81); and again,
the possible discovery of the nature and the contents of God's
revelation to the non-Christian through the work both of creation
and history (p. 71).

It will always remain difficult to understand the nature, contents and methods of pre-evangelization if one does not start from
the facts. Only after having reviewed a large number of case-
studies will a missiologist be able to say or write something valuable on the topic. The experiments missionaries have done and are
doing in this field are of primary importance. Fortunately, in our
day quite a number of them have written down their experiences,
like J. Dournes, M.E.P. (Jörai, South Vietnam), Dr. A.
Lukesch, S.V.D. (Kayapó Indians in Brazil), H. Gravrand C.S.Sp.
(Sérères, Senegal), Pl. Tempels, O.F.M. (Bantus, Congo-Léo),
D. Nothomb, P.B. (Rwanda), A. Kagame (Rwanda), V. Mulago
(Bantus, Rwanda, Burundi, Congo-Léo), W.L. King (Buddhists,
Burma), R. Panikkar (Hindus, India) and A. Peyriguère (Mus-
lims, Morocco). From these and other studies a missiologist and
a missionary can learn much about the first stage of his work, pre-
evangelization, the first step toward the self-realization of the
Church in local Churches through a patient dialogue between
Christianity and other religions, which is perhaps a better description of the missionary activity than conversion of souls or planting
the Church.

Father Spae's study (whose book is the subject of this article)
serves as an example of a case-study on pre-evangelization. It
comes from Japan and is the fruit of long studies and of years of
missionary activity. The material of the book has been previously
published in various magazines, mainly in *The Japan Missionary
Bulletin*. Moreover, the first part was printed in Tokyo, in 1964,
under the title *Pre-catechetics for Japan*. Only minor changes
have been added to the present work. Two more volumes are

---

[1] Spae, Joseph J., C.I.C.M., Ph.D. *Christian Corridors to Japan*,
(Tokyo: Oriens Institute for Religious Research, 1965), 265 pp.

promised in the preface, one on moral notions and the other on dogmatic concepts in Japanese culture and in Christianity.

Christian Corridors to Japan is the first important publication of the Oriens Institute for Religious Research in Tokyo of which Father Spae is director. Some information about the Oriens Institute will help us understand the author's motives.

For 20 years there has been complete religious freedom in Japan; the first response of the Catholic Church to the new situation was an increase in the number of priest-missionaries. In 1963 there were 1,223 foreign and 522 Japanese priests, 1,117 foreign and 3,886 Japanese religious sisters, and 179 foreign and 250 Japanese lay brothers. (Cf. J.J. Spae, C.I.C.M., *Catholicism in Japan: A Sociological Study* (Tokyo, 1963), p. 79. The Catholic population in that year totalled 308,814.

Still, there is some *malaise* in the Church. Frequently one can hear the following complaints: the average missionary's knowledge of Japan and of its language does not make a great impression upon the people. Experts are lacking and there is little or no collaboration among the many orders and congregations working in Japan. Language schools for missionaries seem to be inadequate as they barely equip one to read a newspaper. Many schools of all kinds have been erected, big churches have been built and there is a rush into the direct apostolate; but administration endangers pastoral work. There is a lack of planning in these various works and there is not much contact with the real Japan, although (according to non-Christian Japanese) the future of the Catholic Church should be bright due to the present state of ferment within Japanese society. The Catholic Church still seems to be a small Christian sect among 136 others in the country.

The following ideas were presented by Father Spae in 1964 in his brochure *Japans Pleidooi voor een wetenschappelijk Apostolaat,* which contains articles taken from *Kerk en Missie,* nn. 153, 154 and 156 (Brussels, 1964). Missionaries in Japan and in many other countries are in need of a regional institute of religious research and planning. The erection of such an institute should be a joint venture of ecclesiastical authorities and religious superiors. Father Spae foresees that the work of regional institutes should be coordinated and encouraged by a central institute attached to a Catholic university, which should at the same time train specialists in various fields of knowledge. However, the final aim of this specialization should be a pastoral or missiological one.

We agree with Father Spae's thesis that this scientific approach through specialization, research and planning in regional and central institutes is a primary task of the Secretariat for non-Christians erected at Rome in 1964. This too will be a work of pre-evangelization. It was against this background that in 1964 the Oriens Institute for Religious Research was started in Tokyo by the priests of the Immaculate Heart of Mary (Scheut); the protector of this institute is His Eminence Cardinal Doi of Tokyo. The main program of the institute is to make Japan known to the Church and the Church to Japan. The cleavage between both is now perhaps being bridged by research on the great ideologies that influence leading personalities (90% of whom live in Tokyo), by developing modern techniques of communication between Catholic and non-Christian intellectuals, by setting up a program of higher missiological studies for missionaries who returned to Japan after their first leave and by publishing six magazines. For those who want to know why these ventures were put on the program of Oriens, *Christian Corridors to Japan* will give the answer.

This publication consists of three parts. A short survey of its contents, together with a few critical remarks, is in order.

Part I is entitled "Pre-Catechetics for Japan". According to the author the revealed content of catechetics is universal, the method of catechetics is both universal and specific, but the human dimension, the human condition of him to whom the message is proclaimed is strictly specific (in our case Japanese). Content and method can be learned from handbooks, but there is as yet no description of the religious anthropology of Japan written from a catechetical point of view. The Church has still to discover the specific vocation of Japanese culture and religiosity. Only after this has been discovered can a clearer idea of God's approach to Japan and Japan's approach to God be observed.

This is a positive approach; the author is obviously a defender of the thesis that Christianity is meant to be the fulfillment of other religions. This view presupposes a sound knowledge of, and a deep participation in, the fundamental religious aspirations of Japan. Only in this way will a missionary understand that in all things the action of God, creator, governor and redeemer is present, and he will also discover to what degree all things are subject through sin to distortion and corruption. It is here that the dialogue between Christianity and Japan starts; hence, the need for a pre-catechetical language attuned to the mind and the heart of Japan and for a basic methodology of the presentation of Christianity to Japan, which the author calls pre-apologetics.

Pre-apologetics is the revelation of man's basic tendencies to the non-Christian and the demonstration that they can find fulfillment only in God. These basic tendencies are truth, goodness and happiness; they are to be found also in Buddhism, and they have deeply influenced Japanese religiosity. The author illustrates this point by many examples. Once these tendencies have been awakened, the hearer has become a listener, the spectator a sympathizer and he searches for a social system or a religion by which he can find fulfillment. For this reason Communism and the many new religions of Japan appeal to the people. It is the task of apologetics to demonstrate that the divine (which is truth, goodness and happiness) manifests itself in an historical phenomenon, the Catholic Church.

Next, Father Spae treats of the pre-catechumenate which corresponds to pre-catechesis; he discusses issues such as individual or group instruction, the method and the climate of the pre-catechumenate and the attitude of the catechist (ideally every Catholic). The first part of Spae's book concludes with some observations on the catechumenate in Japan, followed by two appendices.

The first part of *Christian Corridors to Japan* is perhaps the weak part of the book. It is striking that the author does not use the word "pre-evangelization" in the substance of it. Only in the second appendix does he give a definition of the term: "influencing, in the name of the Gospel, everything (milieus and personal situations) which conditions the attention to the kerygma and facilitates access to the faith by individuals and groups" (p. 67). Spae then gives a definition of evangelization, and it appears that both pre-catechetics and catechetics are understood by him to belong to it. Evangelization, however, is intended in his opinion to bring the non-believer to conversion and thence to baptism. The distinction between pre-evangelization and evangelization is to be found in the fact that the first is directed to the masses and that it is used in an occasional way whereas the second is done in a more or less personal and organized way. Therefore, both in the stage of pre-evangelization and in that of pre-catechetics the purpose of leading man to conversion and to baptism is manifest.

This brings us to ask: why put "pre" in front of all these terms? There seems to be no reason for it: And yet implicitly Father Spae is pleading for a special stage in the approach to non-Christians, the stage of penetrating deeply into the fundamental religious aspirations of a people through study, research and participation. In order to achieve this, however, it is necessary to be patient—perhaps for many years—and to wait till the moment arrives when one discovers God's ways of salvation through the religion of the other. This patience will be abundantly rewarded only if the basis for a profound dialogue on the salvific meaning of Christianity for the other religion is established, and only if Christianity can be born again or incarnated in a new culture. This stage of penetration into the mind and the heart of the non-Christians could be called pre-evangelization or the very initial stage of the dialogue. I agree with Grasso and Nebrada that the next two stages are the kerygma and catechesis.

In the preface Father Spae asks for fraternal criticism. My idea of pre-evangelization has been derived from the many case-studies mentioned in the beginning, for I consider this a practical way to arrive at a description of pre-evangelization.

It is striking that the second and the third part of Spae's book do not suffer from inadequate terms. Here Spae is a master in the field, his own field of Japanology, sociology and psychology of non-Western peoples. In the second part the reader will find interesting studies about the population problem, the lack of charitable institutions for those in need, Japan's middle class, Japan's youth in transition, the Japanese intellectuals and the new type Japanese. Observing Japanese society in continuous change, Spae analyzes with great competence the forces that are at work in the new Japan. Moreover, he points the way to missionaries who should have vital contacts with those new forces. Spae's ideal and the inspiration (which gave birth to the Oriens Institute) to bring the Church into contact with the real Japan are fully explained here.

The problems treated in the second part seem to lead to points of contact with Christianity. Leading personalities in non-Christian Japan are asking the Church to guide them through these intricate questions. The answer, however, does not depend on the Church in Japan only, but mainly on the World-Church. The need for a central institute for religious research next to regional centers is well illustrated by Dr. Spae.

The third part is entitled "The Meeting of Culture and Religion". It is noteworthy that the literature mentioned in the notes of the twelve chapters of this part is astonishingly rich. Comprising more than half the book, these chapters deal with the nature of Japanese theology, the problem of integration of Christian and Japanese values, the nature, method and prospects of a dialogue between all the Christians in Japan and between Christians and non-Christians (the smaller and the greater dialogue), the phenomenology of conversion, the various paths along which some Japanese meandered to the Church, a study of the fundamental religious aspirations at work in the popular new religions of Japan, Japanese psychology and religious life, and finally, the need for missionary research for Japan together with a program for the Oriens Institute.

Part III is an exemplary case-study in pre-evangelization for Japan. While Part II is a study of Christianity and Japan's social

problem, Part III is directly concerned with the encounter of religions. Sociology, psychology and the phenomenology of religion
are the tools preparing a missionary for this meeting of religions,
but the ultimate aim of applying these sciences to the religious
situation in Japan is not that of a sociologist, a psychologist or a
phenomenologist. The ultimate purpose is the discovery of God's
salvific action in the pre-Christian Japan or the discovery of how
this pre-Christian Japan is an evangelical preparation (also called
the Old Testament) for the manifest coming of Christianity. A
missionary arriving in Japan—or elsewhere—does not enter into
a void, for it is his privilege to meet the grace of God already at
work in a particular people. God sends him to meet himself—an
enriching encounter for both the Church and the pre-Christian
religion.

Spae reproduces the rather abstract dogmatic theses of Karl
Rahner on the relation of Christianity to other religions, but
thanks to Spae's knowledge of, and penetration into, the Japanese
mind and heart he is able to throw new light on the question. By
starting from reality, from a concrete description of God's salvific
action among a people, the dogmatic theses should be tested in
order to correct, improve or justify them. Here we find the true
task of missiology and the difference between missiology and dogmatic theology.

Only case-studies can help us in this field and Spae's book
should be read by missiologists and missionaries in Japan and
elsewhere. His positive approach to the many new religions originating recently in Japan is most encouraging. We hope that this
view will deeply alter the attitude of missionaries in Japan toward
these religions, for they indicate a religious dynamism in the midst
of a rapidly developed society. The title of Chapter 10 in Part III
serves as a significant manifestation of a new Christian awareness
in investigating "Clues to the Spirit of Japan's Popular Religions".

BIOGRAPHICAL NOTES

TEODORO JIMÉNEZ-URRESTI: Born April 1, 1924 in Bilbao, Spain, and ordained for that diocese in 1949. Studies at the Gregorian and the Lateran Universities in Rome led to the licentiate in dogmatic theology and the doctorate in canon law and Roman law. At present he is a Professor of Dogmatic Theology and Diocesan General Pro-vicar. His publications include *Estado e Iglesia* (Victoria, 1958) and *Binomio "Primado-Episcopado"* (Madrid, 1962), and numerous contributions to scholarly journals.

TOMAS GARCIA BARBERENA: Born September 12, 1911, he was ordained for the Diocese of Ciudad Real in 1935. After studies at the Pontifical Lateran University and the University of Salamanca, he received his doctorate in canon law in 1947. At present he is Professor of Canon Law at the University of Salamanca, and a contributor to the journal *Revista Español de Derecho Canónico*.

MANUEL BONET: Born November 1, 1913, he was ordained for the diocese of Barcelona. He received his doctorate in civil and canon law and his licentiate in theology after studying at the Gregorian and the Lateran Universities, and the Jesuit University of Catalonia. He is a Professor at the Seminary of Barcelona, a Consultant of the Rota, and a Secretary on the Conciliar Commission on the Sacraments. He is the founder of the journal *Revista Español de Derecho Canónico* and the author of numerous articles.

JOSEPH HAJJAR: Born January 24, 1923 in Damascus, Syria, and ordained for the diocese of Damascus in 1946. He attended the Major Seminary of St. Anne in Jerusalem, and the Pontifical Lateran University in Rome where he received his doctorate *"in utroque jure"*. He is Professor of Ecclesiastical History and of Law at the same Major Seminary of St. Anne, and is also the permanent Secretary of the Annual Synod of the Greek-Melchite Catholic Patriarchate. His publications, too numerous to list fully, include frequent contributions to the journal *Proche-Orient Chrétien*, and "La collégialité épiscopale dans la tradition orientale," in *l'Eglise de Vatican II*.

WILHELM DE VRIES: Born May 26, 1904 in Saarbrücken, West Germany. He became a Jesuit and was ordained in 1932. He has studied at the Oriental Pontifical Institute in Rome and at St. Joseph's University in Beirut, Lebanon, obtaining his doctorate in Oriental ecclesiastical science. His important study, *Rom und die Patriarchate des Ostens*, appeared in 1963, and he is a regular contributor to scholarly journals. Since 1939, he has been a Professor at the Oriental Pontifical Institute in Rome.

WILLY ONCLIN: Born February 22, 1905 in Hamont, Belgium, he was ordained for the Diocese of Liège in 1929. Studies at the Catholic University of Louvain led to the doctorate in law in 1934 and the doctorate in canon law in 1948. He has been Professor of Canon Law at the University of Louvain since 1938, and since 1958 Professor on the Faculty of Law at the University of Nijmegen. The author of many articles, his most recent contribution was: "Membres de l'Eglise, personnes dans l'Eglise," in *L'Année canonique*; other articles have appeared in *Ephemerides Theologicae Lovanienses* and *Apollinaris*.

PETRUS HUIZING, S. J.: Born February 22, 1911, he became a Jesuit and was ordained in 1942. After studying at the University of Louvain, the Gregorian University in Rome, and at the University of Munich, he received his doctorate in civil law in 1938, and in canon law in 1947. From 1946-52 he was Professor of Canon Law at the University of Maastricht, and then from 1952-64 at the Gregorian University in Rome.

IVAN ŽUŽEK, S. J.: Born September 2, 1924 in Ljubljana, Yugoslavia. He became a Jesuit and was ordained in 1955. He pursued his studies at the Pontifical Oriental Institute, and then received a licentiate in canon law at the Gregorian University. He has been Professor of Oriental Canon Law at the Oriental Institute since 1963. His publications include: *Kormčaja kniga. Studies on the Chief Code of Russian Canon Law*, and contributions to *Orientalia Christiana Periodica*.

RENÉ LAURENTIN: Born October 19, 1917 in France, he was ordained for the diocese of Angers in 1946. He studied at the Institut Catholique in Paris where he was awarded a doctorate in literature in 1952 and a doctorate in theology in 1953. A *peritus* at Vatican Council II, he is presently Professor at the Catholic University in Angers. Among his numerous works are: *Marie, l'Eglise et le Sacerdoce* 2 Vols. (1953) and *L'enjeu du Concile, Bilans des Sessions*, as well as articles appearing in *Vie spirituelle* and *Revue des sciences philosophique et theologique*.

ARNULF CAMPS, O. F. M.: Born February 1, 1925 at Eindhoven in the Netherlands, he entered the Franciscans and was ordained in 1950. After studying missiology at the Catholic University of Nijmegen and the Catholic University in Fribourg, Switzerland, he earned his doctorate in 1957. Research in the Middle East, Pakistan, India and Ceylon followed four years as Professor of Islamology, Missiology and Church History at the Regional Seminary of West Pakistan. At present he is Professor of Missiology at the Catholic University of Nijmegen. His articles have appeared in many journals, among them: *Neue Zeitschrift für Missionswissenschaft, Studia Orientalia*, and *Oecumene*.

International Publishers of CONCILIUM

ENGLISH EDITION
Paulist Press
Glen Rock, N. J., U.S.A.

Burns & Oates Ltd.
25 Ashley Place
London, S.W.1

DUTCH EDITION
Uitgeverij Paul Brand, N. V.
Hilversum, Netherlands

FRENCH EDITION
Maison Mame
Tours/Paris, France

GERMAN EDITION
Verlagsanstalt Benziger & Co., A.G.
Einsiedeln, Switzerland

Matthias Grunewald-Verlag
Mainz, W. Germany

SPANISH EDITION
Ediciones Guadarrama
Madrid, Spain

PORTUGUESE EDITION
Livraria Morais Editora, Ltda.
Lisbon, Portugal

ITALIAN EDITION
Editrice Queriniana
Brescia, Italy